"A powerful book! Most books like this are inspirational; *Character Works* is life changing."

Mike Kolen
NBC Securities, Inc. and
Former linebacker for the Miami Dolphins

"Nix's book is a powerful tool for those seeking to find fulfillment in both their professional and personal lives. While others dally with the 'secrets of success,' Bill Nix gets to the core of the issue...character! If you want to get off life's treadmill, begin enjoying your interactions with the people around you, and make a substantive, positive contribution to our society, read this book!"

General C.C. Krulak
Commandant of the United States Marine Corps

"Bill Nix understands the issue of the day—character, and he offers this insightful and practical book for anyone who desires greater character of themselves and others. I highly recommend *Character Works*."

Tom Landry
Former Head Coach, Dallas Cowboys

"*Character Works* is a practice guide to understanding what character is and why it is important. Bill Nix explains in a sensible, not preachy way how to recognizes it in others and exhibit it in our own everyday lives."

Pat Noland
President, Justice Fellowship

"I find that *Character Works* addresses a much-neglected attribute in our present culture, that of character. William Nix does an excellent job of not only showing what character is but also of illustrating how it plays out in the daily events of our lives. Sometimes we are unaware of character issues that impact us greatly. I recommend the book."

Tom Osborne
Former Head Football Coach, University of Nebraska

"Bill Nix's book *Character Works* is on target! We need more character in America and not more characters."

Dal Shealy
President/CEO, Fellowship of Christian Athletes

"We live in a culture that says character is separate from competence on the job. My good friend, Bill Nix, reminds us that without character, there is no competence. Many books stress character in your private life. This book encourages you to live out a life of character in your workplace."

John Trent
Encouraging Words

"May the 21st century begin with *Character Works* and with the William Nixes in our country, who live character, breath character, practice character, and communicate character effectivey to all of us."

Joe White
President, Kanakuk Kamps, Inc.

Character WORKS

William H. Nix

B&H BUSINESS

Nashville, Tennessee

0-8054-1653-6

Published by Broadman & Holman Publishers, Nashville, Tennessee
Editorial Team: Leonard G. Goss, John Landers, Sandra Bryer
Page Design and Typesetting: TF Designs, Mount Juliet, Tennessee

Dewey Decimal Classification: 248
Subject Heading: BUSINESS ETHICS

Unless otherwise noted, Scripture quotations are from the Holy Bible,
New International Version, © copyright 1973, 1978, 1984.
Passages marked NKJV are from the
New King James Version, copyright © 1979, 1980, 1982,
Thomas Nelson, Inc., Publishers.

Library of Congress Cataloging-in-Publication Data

Nix, William, 1959—
    Character works / by William H. Nix
        p. cm.
    Includes bibliographical references
    ISBN 0-8054-1653-6
        1. Businesspeople—Religious life. 2. Christian ethics. 3. Business ethics.
    4. Character.
    I. Title.
    BV4596.B8N58 1999
    248.8'8—dc21   99—28284
                                                              CIP

1 2 3 4 5 03 02 01 00 99

To my precious wife,
Teri,
and our wonderful children,
Lauren, Will, and Mary Grayson.
You continue to joyfully bless
and enrich my life in so many ways.
I love you.

To my loving mother,
Hazel Nix
and in special memory of my dad,
Earl Nix.
Your lives, marked by character,
have compelled so many of us
to live at a higher standard.
Thank you for living such a legacy.
I love you.

Contents

Applying the Character Equation

INTRODUCTION

Is Character the Issue?

ifty minutes into the committee meeting of a fine organization my still small voice awakened me asking, "What does this meeting, and this committee for that matter, have to do with anything of significance to me?" The same question had haunted me throughout my career—first in my work as an investment banker, later as a mortgage banker. For many years I wandered through life searching for a connection between my purpose in life and my practice of life. Life was confusing in those days because I felt I understood my purpose but failed to see how my work and other areas of my life related to it. I could not connect the dots in this picture of my life.

I experienced a life-changing God-incidence at my mortgage banking office that led to several discoveries. A God-incidence is, for me, what others may call coincidence.

WHAT IS CHARACTER?

First I discovered an expanded definition of *character*. Webster defines *character* as "the total quality of a person's behavior." Character is often thought of as honesty and integrity. By this commonly accepted definition, character is limited to the practice of life, the way we live. But character is much more. Character also includes why we live, our purpose in life. My expanded definition of character reads, "The total quality of a person's behavior leading to the fulfillment of that person's purpose." Stated simply, character is the strength to practice a purposeful life.

HOW ARE CHARACTER, PURPOSE, AND PRACTICE CONNECTED?

Next, I discovered character is a choice. We all have a purpose in life and are endowed with the abilities, passion, and relationships required to fulfill

1

that purpose. Character gives us strength to make tough choices in the practice of our life that lead to the realization of the purpose of our life.

When the link between purpose and practice is broken, we often make bad choices. Perhaps you know someone who drifts according to cultural winds. Your friend may have no sense of purpose in life. Maybe you have a friend whose purpose in life is clear, but that purpose is linked to a poor practice of life. Your friend's purpose may be to climb the corporate ladder, and the resulting practice of life includes stepping on anyone in the way. Your friend may be following the wrong purpose.

Character is produced and matured when we make the connection between our purpose and our practice. The character equation helps us remember the importance of both purpose and practice:

$$Character = Purpose \times Practice$$

We can know our purpose but never practice it. Consider the character equation in the context of a football team. On the day the players report, the coach gives a stirring speech about the purpose of the team: "We are going all the way to the Super Bowl." The guys are fired up by the hope of wearing a Super Bowl ring. Then the coach turns to the practice schedule saying: "Our first game is in one month. Be here an hour before the game. In the meantime, have fun, satisfy your own desires, do not worry about getting any sleep or staying in shape." Their character equation looks like this:

$$Character = Purpose \times Practice$$
$$0 = 100 \times 0$$

The team members know their purpose, but their failure to practice it produces zero character.

On the other hand, imagine a coach practicing his football team every day but never establishing a purpose (such as winning the Super Bowl). All week the team practices drill after drill, then on game day the coach says, "OK, just get out there and play." The team's practice does not amount to much because their practice did not lead to a purpose. In this instance, their character equation looks like this:

$$Character = Purpose \times Practice$$
$$0 = 0 \times 100$$

Many people live life the same way. I have, and I believe you have also. I have wandered through phases of my life sensing a purpose but still pursuing many of the things in life that did not support that purpose. In a word,

I was selfish. Many people live good, moral lives but have no sense of purpose. They are known as good people, but who are they becoming? These people have no direction, and their lives do not amount to much.

The New Testament writer Paul put it this way, "Therefore, I urge you, brothers, in view of God's mercy, to offer your bodies as living sacrifices, holy and pleasing to God—this is your spiritual act of worship. Do not conform any longer to the pattern of this world, but be transformed by the renewing of your mind. Then you will be able to test and approve what God's will is—his good, pleasing and perfect will" (Rom. 12:1–2). In effect, Paul was saying the more we present ourselves as living sacrifices (that is, our practice of life) the more we will understand why we live (that is, our purpose in life). Then the more we understand our purpose in life, the corresponding practice of life becomes more natural; the more naturally we practice life, the more we understand our purpose.

Choosing to practice a purposeful life is like lifting weights. The more repetitions lifted of a weight, the stronger we become. The stronger we become, the greater weight we can lift. Choosing to practice a purposeful life is an act of character. Practicing a purposeful life strengthens our character muscle.

When I applied these discoveries in my life, I experienced the life-changing power of character. A person of character enjoys an exponentially better life marked by fulfillment, stability, and meaning.

Perhaps you are weary from the demands of overcommitment. People of character live with joy because they know taking that time moves them in the direction of their purpose. People who have no sense of purpose do not have time to stop and enjoy life because they are pursuing all the latest fads. If the urgent demands of the day have robbed you of the joy of the journey, keep reading.

Maybe you feel unsettled by life's unpleasant surprises. People of character face and address the hard things in life because they know their purpose waits on the other side of the difficulty. People who have no purpose avoid—put off—life's difficult moments because they do not see the possibility for good that can come from confronting difficult issues. Purpose gives meaning to the difficulty along the way. Perhaps you feel too soft to tackle life's hard things. Read on.

Many people harbor anger and resentment because others have achieved their definition of success. People of character have a clear picture of their direction, and they are satisfied with it, which explains why they so easily and often serve others. A person whose practice of life is selfish is never satisfied. Maybe you feel others have passed you in the race of life. Perhaps you are running the wrong race. Keep reading.

Our society continues to water down the meaning of old-fashioned honesty and truthfulness. People of character know they are headed to a better place in life so the opportunities for ill-gotten gain are not tempting. People whose practice of life leads to a breach of their integrity never arrive at a better place. In fact they are headed in the direction of trouble. If you are traveling down this road, stop and read for a new direction.

WHAT CAN YOU EXPECT IN THIS BOOK?

I wrote this book to help myself and others become people of character. The character equation serves as the book's framework. Chapters 1 through 3 relate to purpose. There you will find practical ways to help you understand your unique purpose in life. Chapters 4 through 13 relate to our practice of life. This section provides ten character-building practices. You will find stories of people who offer illustrations of the practice. Some of their stories are inspiring, and their actions can be replicated in your life. Others instruct us in what not to do.

Chapters 14 through 20 describe how purpose and practice can produce character in six real-life dilemmas that confront you every day. From dealing with a difficult boss, employee, or coworker; to managing your anger; to handling your successes and failures, this section takes the character equation and helps you apply its meaning where the rubber meets the road in your life at work, at home, and wherever you may be.

You may consider some of my points and perspectives to be common knowledge—my contention that purpose and practice are linked, for instance. Though you may consider this thought to be common knowledge, is it common practice in your life? This book will help you solve the character equation by providing helpful ways to discover and understand your unique purpose and practical ideas to translate your purpose into practice.

Now is the time to solve the character equation and enjoy the exponentially positive life change that awaits.

ONE

Purposeful Problems

*L*ike any other day I awoke at 6:00 A.M. and started a routine which took me to my office at the mortgage company at 7:45 A.M. It appeared to be a typical day, and that was good because typical, predictable days are a banker's desire. Appearances, as I learned once again that day, can be deceiving.

8:00 A.M.

Business consolidations, mergers, and buyouts are common in the banking industry. At the mortgage company, we were rarely surprised when two banks announced their marriage, but each announcement brought a blanket of stress to our workplace.

Putting two companies together may increase market share. Buying out a supplier may give the purchaser juicier profit margins. Merging with a competitor could result in greater efficiency as people in duplicate roles are laid off. People employed in the banking industry often become enraged by the stress caused by the fear of losing their jobs due to merger mania.

The first person to greet me on this soon-to-be-atypical day was one of our managers, Marcia, who had heard we were being acquired by a competing banking institution. Marcia had taken the rumor as fact and concluded her job was history. I calmed her fear with the assuring words that we were not the apple of that other bank's corporate eye. She left my office ready to tackle the day.

8:25 A.M.

Soon after Marcia, the merger-maimed manager, turned the corner from my office, the company's personnel director came in for a visit. She began to replay the conversation she had earlier with an obstetrician. The physician was calling to ask us to accommodate the special medical needs of his patient and our employee, Leah. His request was simple. Allow Leah to prop her feet up at her desk and give her one extra fifteen-minute break during the afternoon. After a moment of discussion, I agreed that we should bend the rules for Leah. After all, I would hope my employer would accommodate me if I had made a reasonable request due to a medical necessity.

9:02 A.M.

Just as the personnel director was leaving, a manager hurried in bearing the news of a chronic problem of slowness. An employee, Tommy, showed up late for work for the umpteenth time. What do you do with an employee or coworker when a description of "slow as molasses" would be an improvement? In this case, we chose a thorough discussion with Tommy as one last chance.

9:30 A.M.

Until this moment, the day was fairly typical. That changed when I answered the phone. The voice on the other end, speaking low, said, "Can you come to my office? I have to talk with you now!" The caller's urgency immediately compelled me out the door and a few floors down. She was waiting, her hand on the doorknob, when I crossed the threshold of her office. "Why the cloak and dagger?" I asked, somewhat annoyed by the suspense of it all. Remember that bankers do not like surprises.

Her message was a surprise—the kind of surprise that confirmed why bankers do not like them. Her surprise, "I have been harassed by a coworker, sexually!" She went on: "I have handwritten notes and a tape recording to prove it. My lawyer said to speak with you about it. What are you going to do?"

10:35 A.M.

I was back in my office weighing what action to take regarding the surprise of my earlier meeting, When Aubrey, the manager of our internal audit department, entered my office. Internal auditors do not just drop in for a cup of coffee. Their presence, especially when it is unexpected, usually means one thing—trouble.

After the shock of my surprise meeting, I was ready to hear just about anything, or so I thought. "We have a problem," he began. "We have a consistent error in our computer system," he continued. Knowing the area of the system in question, I quickly determined the problem could cost several million dollars. Aubrey breezed out the doorway of my office about the time my finger hit the total key on my calculator, revealing the sum of the mistake.

11:20 A.M.

By this point of the day, I reasoned my best work could be accomplished out of the office. I was preparing to leave for some fresh air and time of reflection when the phone rang again. I thought about just letting it ring, but I answered it curtly. More surprises. Checks had been stolen from a branch office, and they were being cashed around town. I left for lunch feeling like I had spent a week at the office that morning.

11:35 A.M.

With my car in sight, I knew I was close to escaping the difficulty of the morning. I was close, but I was still far away! Their loud words drew the attention of everyone passing by, especially me, since Jane and Tom were managers who reported to me. Tom and Jane were fighting like two kids on the playground. The striped shirt I was wearing that day seemed appropriate as I refereed their fight.

1:30 P.M.

Returning to the office from a much-needed lunch break, I reasoned the afternoon would surely redeem the morning. I had been in the office only five minutes when, once again, the phone rang. I answered, confident the news would be good. It was not. Claire, an employee in the microfilm department, had collapsed. Skipping three steps at a time, I rushed down four floors to the scene. The paramedics were arriving at the same moment. Claire had jammed her hand in a document feeder, and the pain caused her to faint. Smelling salts revived Claire, and she was transported to a nearby hospital.

2:15 P.M.

Just as I was putting the finishing touches on my resignation, I heard a knock at the door. "What is your problem?" I asked my visitor, expecting more trouble. But this visitor must have been an angel sent to brighten my day.

Iris managed the microfilm department. She began, "I know the timing of this visit is not exactly perfect given what just happened with Claire." I filled the space of her pause saying, "Go on." Iris got right to the point, "Well, I attended a technology conference recently and learned about imaging. If we invest in imaging, we can downsize my department."

I asked Iris to repeat her words. Could it be? This day was about crisis. This was a hard day, but into this day of difficulty came a cool breeze of something positive. Iris, not knowing how downsizing might affect her, brought to my attention a way to become more efficient. *Maybe there is hope*, I thought as I crumpled up my resignation and deposited it in the trash.

2:45 P.M.

Finally, this dark day had turned bright. The difficulty had ended. The storm had passed, right? Our personnel director dropped in. As with internal auditors, an unexpected visit from a personnel director often means trouble. The warmth I felt from the visit with Iris turned cold in the darkness of the news. One of our young men, Clarence, had tested positive for cocaine. Unfortunately, about 6 percent of our people regularly tested positive for an illegal drug. That percentage may seem low, but it means another person has fallen prey to that evil.

3:17 P.M.

When it rains it pours, and it seemed like a flood by mid-afternoon. Darla was on the phone from home requesting a one-week vacation. I knew Darla. I knew her weaknesses; and the slur of her words told me she, like her coworker Clarence, had succumbed. Darla was an alcoholic who had fallen off the wagon. Her request for a week off meant she wanted to lay out and drink.

4:25 P.M.

Hearing footsteps outside my office, I spun around in my chair to see five women, all coworkers in the same department, asking for a moment of my time. These women were there to report on the unfair practice of our personnel department. One of their coworkers was granted a special privilege, and this group felt either they should be granted the same privilege or their coworker should lose it. As if the events of the day had not ganged up on me already, now I had five disgruntled employees.

5:15 P.M.

I pulled the crumpled resignation from my trash can. Part of me wanted to lay it on my boss's desk, but another part of me wanted to trash it and meet head-on the challenges presented that day. I found the challenge more compelling. I sensed the day's events would become a blessing—that this clear contrast between the way we often live at work and the way we should and could live at work would become a great teacher. It did.

This day woke me to the root cause of the problems so many of us face every day. In the haze of the awakening, I realized that many of our work-related productivity and relationship problems are the result of the unresolved problems faced by the individuals in our workplace.

THE PROBLEM

SYMPTOMS

Call it intuition or perhaps insight gained from years of experience, but I sensed a revelation was imminent. A diagnosis of the cause of my unforgettable day was about to become clear.

Reflecting on that day, a common thread seemed to weave its way through most of the circumstances. Most of the people I encountered that day were simply going through the motions of life. My coworkers were expending little, if any, creative or physical energy. To be blunt, they were doing just enough to get by.

When people are chronically late to work, they are just going through the motions of life. Redundant error is a clear indication the error-maker is expending little if any creative or physical energy. Leaving checks out, making their theft an easy crime is at best doing just enough to get by. A theme had emerged.

My coworkers were coasting through life, especially life at work. Like so many people, my coworkers seemed resigned to whatever happened as if they could do nothing to effect a positive outcome in life. Therefore, they acted on whatever whim entered their minds. They engaged in whatever seemed gratifying at the moment. Whatever provided the quickest fix to a problem, however short-lived it may be, they applied like a Band-Aid.

That explained why Darla and Clarence covered their deeper problems with alcohol and drugs. That explained why my coworker gave into a sexual sickness and harassed his female colleague instead of seeking the cure. That explained why five women allowed selfish instincts to suppress the goodness in their hearts by attempting to thwart our effort to meet the need of a coworker.

All of these people were coasting, resigned to the often-strong winds of life. Wearing an irritating smirk that says "whatever," these people float along, dodging responsibility for their lives. The failure to accept personal

9

responsibility leaves people longing for that missing something. Dodging responsibility creates in most of us a gnawing ache deep in our souls. That pain compels some people to face the ultimate disease and find the cure. Others, however, respond to the pain by becoming more cynical and even less responsible.

My diagnosis was confirmed when I learned the problem was evident in workplaces across the country. Wilson Learning Corporation commissioned a study of the subject and found that 80 percent of the respondents admitted they were "inactive," meaning they were just doing their job but were unwilling to expend their energy.[1] My experience was not unique at all. In fact, the disease that plagued my coworkers had infected the population in epidemic proportions.

Henry David Thoreau aptly described this illness when he wrote, "What is called resignation is confirmed desperation."[2] Though it is quiet, desperation leads one to cry out for help by being consistently late for work. Persons desperately seeking to ease that gnawing pain pursue so much activity away from work that they collapse at work. Out of desperation we risk our lives for the quick high of the moment. Desperation leaves us feeling hopeless, seeing no way out, so we take our vacation to stay home drunk. This quiet desperation whispers the message that our work is really irrelevant, so we effectively resign and fall into a pattern of making careless and costly errors.

We see our desperate coworkers and attribute their behavior to a difficult childhood. Perhaps we see their desperation and incorrectly assume training alone will correct their behavior. We might even conclude that those desperate souls around us are simply people of bad character. These conclusions are the easy way out. By attributing this deeply rooted disease to problems in childhood or solely to a need for training, we only reinforce the desperate person's desire to play the victim. We must address the disease.

THE DISEASE

An attempt could be made to diagnose this disease by focusing on the desperate, ruling out possibilities on a basis of trial and error. The clearest, most accurate diagnosis, however, can be made by focusing on the responsible—that 20 percent who responded as "active" in the Wilson Learning Corporation study.

Why does that group seem content and balanced in life while the desperate flounder? What makes that group punctual? What keeps those with addictive tendencies from giving in? What compels the "active" bunch to master the details while the majority say "whatever"? What does the productive, functioning minority have that their desperate coworkers do not?

The answer to all of these questions is the same; the "active," responsible minority has purpose. The disease that is plaguing our workplaces today is Purpose Deficiency Syndrome. Purpose Deficiency Syndrome manifests itself in many of the ways already mentioned. The desperate are so often too unaware of their problems to recognize them.

People need to see the relevance of their work in order to establish its value. We value that which we view as important. We apply ourselves to that which we view as important. Work becomes relevant, valuable, and important when we understand our personal purpose and how that aligns with our purpose at work.

Some people believe money, or financial gain, is the purpose of work. While there is a practical need for money, it is not a purpose that sustains the health of the individual. In fact, a single-minded pursuit of financial gain can lead to Purpose Deficiency Syndrome. A *Business Week*/Harris study revealed "95% of adults reject the view that a corporation's only role is to make money."[3]

Solomon was one of the wisest men to have lived. Solomon wrote, "Where there is no revelation, the people cast off restraint" (Prov. 29:18). Solomon was saying that when people see no purpose in life they wander aimlessly. That is a good definition of Purpose Deficiency Syndrome. Because work is such a large part of our lives, that is where Purpose Deficiency Syndrome naturally impacts its victims, the desperate.

Purpose Deficiency Syndrome is an infectious disease millions of people take to work every day. The disease can spread in a workplace from one infected, desperate soul to the next. A cure is found in this most unlikely place—the workplace. The workplace is where the symptoms are seen. The workplace bears most of the cost of the disease, and the workplace can help bring purpose to the desperate.

APPLY THE CHARACTER EQUATION
1. List several of your everyday encounters with coworkers or customers that illustrate Purpose Deficiency Syndrome.
2. List ways you have demonstrated Purpose Deficiency Syndrome.

Two

The Cure

WRONG PRESCRIPTIONS

*I*n our fast-paced world we often make judgments too quickly, hoping for solutions overnight. For instance, from that most memorable day at the office, I could have quickly concluded that we had a corporate problem. That quick assessment, however, would not have yielded the solution.

Corporate problems are created by individuals, yet the typical response to workplace problems is with corporate fixes. Total Quality Management (TQM) initiatives seek to solve problems corporately through the development and improvement of processes. Work teams are employed to fix the corporate focus on a task. Policies and procedures are documented in an effort to ensure compliance. TQM, work teams, and policies and procedures are all good; but all fail to address the central cause of workplace problems, which is Purpose Deficiency Syndrome.

The events of my unforgettable day were not the result of a problem at the corporate level. Rather, the problem was at the individual level and came to my attention only after a number of individual problems occurred in a single day. The cure was just around the corner. The cure was found by addressing the needs of the individuals in our workplace.

CHOICE

One of the great gifts in life is the freedom to choose. We are free to choose where we live, whom we live with, when to go to the mall, where we will work, to worship God or not to worship God, to find a cure for Purpose Deficiency Syndrome or to continue wandering aimlessly through life, and on and on. We even choose what we become. The saying, "You are what you eat," applies here. What we become in life is the exact result of the decisions, attitudes, activities, and relationships we choose along the way.

Some people believe fate determines our destiny. Others would say life is a chance existence consisting of haphazard luck. Their view of the world puts no responsibility on the individual to live a purposeful life. "Why take responsibility for anything? There is nothing I could do to change the outcome," they might say. This is the most severe form of Purpose Deficiency Syndrome.

These Purpose Deficiency Syndrome sufferers would tell Clarence, the cocaine addict, "Don't sweat your addiction, Clarence. It is genetics." Genetics can render a person to be more inclined toward addictive behavior, but the person still has the choice to use drugs and the choice to seek help. Addiction to drugs, alcohol, pornography, or anything else is a choice.

The freedom to choose brings with it the mantle of responsibility. True freedom of choice does not exist without responsibility. Responsibility does not exist without a standard or set of standards. It is the standard that creates the need for responsibility. The standard is a person's purpose. Purpose Deficiency Syndrome erases a person's desire for purpose. The ripple effect is predictable. Purpose Deficiency Syndrome creeps in and tricks its victim into believing choice can be enjoyed without responsibility.

Purpose Deficiency Syndrome gives its victim the perspective of Tommy, the tardy employee. Tommy was shocked by his supervisor's reaction. In Tommy's view his tardiness "did not hurt anyone." Clarence believed he could use cocaine without his addiction ever becoming a problem. I believe Purpose Deficiency Syndrome caused famed Houston Rockets star Charles Barkley to declare, "I am not a role model!" By their actions all were saying, "I have the right to choose to be late; to use drugs; to play a high-paid game without having to accept responsibility for my choices." Wrong guys!

I believe Tommy's, Clarence's, and Charles's blatant disregard for responsibility can be linked to Purpose Deficiency Syndrome. Bringing these guys and the millions like them back among the responsible requires a healthy dose of purpose.

FINDING PURPOSE

I have found that a clear understanding of my purpose brings me a sense of fulfillment, stability, and meaning. Most people search their entire lives for these qualities. So many people never experience true fulfillment, stability, and meaning because they fail to find their purpose.

People today tend to look in all the wrong places. The pursuit of wealth is probably the most common place people search for fulfillment, stability, and meaning. Building a big bank account becomes the purpose in life, but soon the thrill of reconciling an ever-growing bank statement fades. Money is a necessary commodity in our society, but money does not bring true, lasting joy and contentment. I know because building wealth was my goal for a number of years. A cold chill engulfed my body the morning I looked in the mirror and said, "So what!" I wanted more than money could buy.

People pursue fulfillment, stability, and meaning in other ways such as occupying a position of power or finding their name in lights. History is full of people who have burned out on, given up on, and checked out of this life angry, bitter, depressed, and disillusioned. Kurt Cobain and his rock group Nirvana topped the charts with their music, yet he committed suicide in 1994 at the age of twenty-seven. Ernest Hemingway, prolific author of classics such as *A Farewell to Arms* and *The Sun Also Rises,* ended his earthly walk on purpose in 1961. These guys probably never understood where to find true fulfillment, stability, and meaning.

THE EQUATION FOR PURPOSE

Fulfillment, stability, and meaning flow from a clear sense of purpose which is found as we apply our abilities to that which we value for the benefit of others. It sounds simple, but defining our specific purpose is not always easy to do. I have expressed the character equation definition of purpose as this formula:

$$\text{Purpose} = (\text{Abilities} + \text{Passion}) \times \text{Relationships}$$

Curing Purpose Deficiency Syndrome in organizations requires each member of that organization to solve the purpose equation. Solving the purpose equation is a process that requires much energy and consideration. Step 1 of the process requires that we understand our unique, inborn, and/or developed abilities. Step 2 is defining our passion. Step 3 acknowledges our relationships.

STEP 1: ABILITIES

No two people are exactly alike. Even identical twins have different fingerprints. Fingerprints are one way you are unique. Abilities are another way you are unique. You were endowed at birth with a special, unique propensity to excel in specific areas. Perhaps you have developed additional skills and abilities as well.

If you are not certain of your abilities, answer the following questions.
1. What activity comes most naturally?
2. What activity is most comfortable?
3. What activity do you most enjoy?
4. In what activity do you see the most accomplishment?
5. In what activity do others most compliment your work?

[handwritten note: I start with where people are & that's good enough]

We often overlook those abilities that come naturally. An evidence of an inborn ability is our level of comfort when using it. Another sign of an inborn ability is the enjoyment we derive from using it. Other people confirm our unique abilities when they comment on or compliment our efforts.

If the questions above have not helped bring clarity to your understanding of your abilities, consider the list below. This list of abilities merely scratches the surface of the many possible abilities you may possess. This list is just a starting place. Feel free to add to it.

Write	Create	Manage	Nurse
Nurture	Counsel	Sing	Cook
Paint	Draw	Build	Challenge
Develop	Discern	Pray	Play
Speak	Talk	Organize	Negotiate
Study	Teach	Research	Act
Lead	Learn	Dance	Encourage

[handwritten: Facilitate]

You are unique. That uniqueness is to be used to understand and accomplish your purpose. If you are a sufferer of Purpose Deficiency Syndrome, you may not know what your unique abilities are, or you may not be applying them.

Your unique abilities may appear to be totally unrelated to your work, but you cannot fully understand your purpose until you understand the uniqueness you bring to all areas of life. A surgeon has the unique ability to work with his or her hands to heal others. A surgeon may find the process of connecting his or her unique abilities to their purpose an easy task, but what about a banker or a truck driver? What about a janitor?

The chairman of the board of a large American company was leaving his corporate headquarters one evening when he encountered the building's janitor, Max. The chairman stopped to speak to Max when he noticed the janitor had a spiral notebook folded in his back pocket. Upon inquiry the boss learned the notebook was full of poetry written by Max. The chairman learned an important truth when he read the janitor's work that evening. The chairman learned that when he hired the janitor the whole person showed

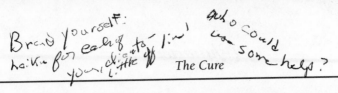
up for work. Work took on new meaning for Max when he realized his unique ability to write poetry was beneficial to his coworkers. Suddenly Max's writing was not some activity disconnected from the huge area of life we call work.

Your unique abilities may not appear to be directly connected to the activity of your job any more than Max's ability to write helped him sweep floors. In time you will learn your true job is your purpose. Stretch your thinking. How are you uniquely gifted? Using the abilities listed above plus any abilities you might add, list three of your unique abilities.

Step 1:   Unique ability 1 *Start where people are as perfect/enough*
Unique ability 2 *draw people into discussion*
Unique ability 3_____

STEP 2: PASSION

You and I may both be uniquely skilled to build, but your level of skill may differ from my level of skill. We share the unique ability to build, but each possesses differing degrees of ability. This principle also applies to our passion. You and I may have an appreciation for the same things, but our passion about those things may vary. For example, we both may have an appreciation for housing as a value we honor, but your passion about housing may be greater than my passion. We both may have an appreciation for the culture, but my passion may be greater than yours. We are both builders, but my passion has led me to apply my unique ability to the culture while your passion has led you to apply your unique ability to building homes.

Understanding our purpose requires that we understand our passion. We allocate time to those things about which we are passionate. We give our energy to those activities that possess our passion. The questions below will help you discover your passion.

1. If you had one day left on earth and could pick just one activity for that day, what would it be?
2. If you had two days and two activities, what would you choose?
3. Now, if you had three days and three activities, what would you choose?
4. What activity occupies most of your mental energy? physical energy?
5. Considering your response to these questions, what difference would your involvement in these activities make? Are you compelled and excited by that difference?

Listed below is a partial list of things about which we may be passionate. Add to the list, but use this to get started uncovering your passion.

Faith	Family	Friendship
World Peace	Personal Growth	Health
Civil Rights	Service	Literacy
Housing	Culture	Environment
Children	Animals	Art
Athletics	Music	Scholarship
Religion	Reading	Education

what would you like to know (handwritten)

Are you suffering from Purpose Deficiency Syndrome? Perhaps you are following a course you do not value. Working in the area of your passion is one evidence you are living out your purpose. Go back to the questions on the previous page, removing any preconceived opinions, then list your top three passions below.

Step 2:   Passion 1_____

Passion 2_____

Passion 3_____

STEP 3: RELATIONSHIPS

Our unique abilities combine with our unique passions, to give us direction that leads to purpose. But abilities and passion alone do not yield purpose. We must ask the third and probably most important question of this process, "For whom is our purpose intended?"

Relationships are the third and most significant component of the purpose equation. The equation sums our abilities and our passion, then multiplies the sum by our relationships. When our abilities are applied to our passion for the benefit of others, purpose is realized.

We are made for relationships. In the Genesis account of creation, the only thing God said was not good was loneliness. "The LORD God said, 'It is not good that man should be alone; I will make him a helper comparable to him'" (Gen. 2:18 NKJV). I believe we are experiencing Purpose Deficiency Syndrome in epidemic proportions because too many of us are lonely.

A friend came to me describing his depression. I hear that a lot. My advice to my friend was simple: "Today, before the sun sets, go and do something kind for someone. Meet someone else's need. Serve someone else in some way." I heard my father give that bit of simple wisdom to a friend of his who was depressed. It worked for my dad's friend. It worked for my friend because serving someone else thrusts the often isolated, lonely, and depressed person into a relationship with another person.

We gain a new, more objective perspective when we help someone. We realize our problems are not as great as we imagined. We acknowledge there are others who will walk with us through our crisis. We realize we do not have to face our problems alone.

We cannot understand our purpose without understanding our relationships. The following questions are offered to help you identify, define, and understand your relationships.

1. For whom or with whom do you enjoy exercising your unique abilities?
2. Who or what is the object of your passion?
3. Who shares your passion?
4. If you had only one more day on earth with only one person, who would you choose?
5. If you had only two more days on earth with only two people, who would you choose?
6. If you had only three more days on earth and could choose three people, who would you choose?

Add to the following list of people with whom you may have relationships.

God	Family	Wife	Husband
Child	Sister	Brother	Father
Mother	Friend	Customer	Employee
Boss	Stockholder	Vendor	Constituent
Grandparent	Neighbor	Pastor	

Are you suffering from Purpose Deficiency Syndrome? Perhaps your purpose equation included self as the relationship variable. You are finding that applying your unique abilities and passion for your exclusive benefit does not produce the fulfillment, stability, and meaning that flow from understanding your purpose. List below the three most important relationships in your life.

Step 3:   Relationship 1_____

Relationship 2_____

Relationship 3_____

YOUR PURPOSE STATEMENT

If we have been given unique abilities and unique passions and if we were endowed with a hunger for relationships from birth, why do we suffer from Purpose Deficiency Syndrome? If these components of purpose exist in us already, why do we fail to see our purpose? I believe it is because we have also been given the gift of choice. We can choose to pursue our purpose, or we can choose to go our own way. We need help making the best choice among the many choices we face everyday. We need a principle around which we can organize our lives so that we will make the choices that will lead us to accomplish our purpose.

A purpose statement is that organizing principle. Organizations have developed corporate mission statements describing their purpose. Yet many of these same organizations suffer from Purpose Deficiency Syndrome because the individual members of the organization fail to see the relevance of their life's work. For an organization's purpose statement to be accomplished, the individual members of that organization need to connect their personal purpose with the purpose of their organization.

Perhaps your organization has a fully developed purpose statement, but you have felt detached from it. Now is the time to connect the dots between your work life, your home life, your spiritual life, etc. The process of developing your personal statement of purpose will help you think through the connection of these areas of your life. You will discover opportunities you never before envisioned. You will see the mundane areas of your life in a new, exciting way. The result will be a statement of purpose that will become the organizing principle of your life.

PURPOSE OF THE PURPOSE STATEMENT

Your purpose statement has at least three purposes of its own. First, your purpose statement will become a guide for making decisions. When faced with major decisions in your work life, personal life, and spiritual life, the purpose statement stands as an unemotional standard. If the activity in question supports and furthers the purpose statement, your decision may be to go with it. Conversely, if the activity does not further your purpose, your best decision may be to pass. Your purpose statement is a guide for making decisions in an increasingly active culture.

Second, your purpose statement provides accountability. Emotions often cause us to make poor decisions. The purpose statement calls you to remember your purpose even when emotions are high. Our choices in life are often confined to good choices versus best choices. When was the last time you were confronted with two options where one option was clearly bad and the other option was clearly good? Most people do not have a clear contrast between decisions. Most people must choose between that which is good and that which is best. Purpose statements then are all the more important. Purpose statements help you distinguish best decisions from good decisions.

Third, purpose statements track our growth. Purpose statements change from time to time as we grow. As we grow as individuals, our understanding of our purpose grows as well. Our purpose has not changed, but our understanding of our purpose has changed. Be ready to enhance your purpose statement as your understanding of your purpose grows.

ELEMENTS OF A STRONG PURPOSE STATEMENT

First, a strong purpose statement should be concise. Less is more! Brevity rather than long-winded dissertations often indicates deeper understanding. The more concise the statement, the easier it will be to remember and the easier it will be to explain to someone else.

Second, a strong purpose statement is compelling in all areas of your life. Your entire life has purpose, so your purpose statement should encompass your entire life. Your understanding of your purpose involves your passion. If your statement does not light the fire of your passion, keep drafting it until the passion is blazing.

Third, a strong purpose statement is clear. You should write your statement so that in one year, and even five years from now, you will remember with clarity exactly what you meant the day you penned the statement.

PUTTING YOUR PURPOSE STATEMENT TOGETHER

Using the words listed in steps 1 through 3, begin drafting a concise, action-oriented statement that answers the question, What is the purpose of my life? As you write and rewrite your statement, you may decide to drop some of the words you have used. For example, my purpose statement reads, "Building faith, family, and friendship."

I used one ability, building, together with three passions—faith, family, and friendship—for the benefit of all the relationships in my life. Now it is your turn. Developing your purpose statement takes time. You will write it and rewrite it many times before your purpose statement is complete. Have fun. Work on it as you read on.

APPLY THE CHARACTER EQUATION

1. Write your purpose statement incorporating the abilities, passions, and relationships you listed in this chapter.
2. Now rewrite the statement making it more concise.
3. Ask a trusted friend to review and critique this statement based on his or her knowledge and understanding of your abilities, passions, and relationships.

THREE

Connecting the Dots

$\mathcal{I}$s your purpose the cure for Purpose Deficiency Syndrome? Understanding your purpose is eternally important, so it is appropriate to put your purpose statement to the test. Testing the validity of your purpose statement means assessing its relevance to your life today and life in the future.

WORK LIFE TODAY

One of the most common causes of Purpose Deficiency Syndrome is the failure to see our work in the context of our purpose. We go to work never realizing how to apply our purpose. Can you achieve your purpose in your current job? These questions may help you.

1. Review the mission/vision/purpose statement of your employer. Does that statement include values or activities that are mutually exclusive to your purpose? If so, maybe a discussion with your employer would be helpful.

2. If no conflict between your purpose and the purpose of your employer exists, how can your personal purpose be realized while supporting the purpose of your employer? Consider my purpose statement, "Building faith, family, and friendship." Can I realize this purpose while being employed at a bank? Yes, remember my God-incidence. That was a day of instruction for me, and through those circumstances my faith grew. Through my responses to their problems, I grew closer to my friends at work. I can build faith, family, and friendship among people while building a bank. Likewise, I can build faith, family, and friendship with people by helping improve workplace environments, which is my work today. My real job, however, is my purpose.

23

Lending money and consulting with companies are simply the venues through which I accomplish my purpose.

You may share my ability to build, but your passion may run high for housing. In that case you may be more inclined to build homes. Building homes is the necessary platform for you to accomplish your purpose. The combination of your abilities and passion will give you direction to the place you apply them for the benefit of others. You should find the common ground between your life's purpose and the purpose of your work. Making this connection will bring new perspective to your eight-to-five grind and serve as a vaccination against Purpose Deficiency Syndrome.

HOME LIFE TODAY

Another cause of Purpose Deficiency Syndrome is the failure to align our life's purpose with the people we love the most, our family. This leads to the feeling we live in at least two separate worlds—our world at work and our world at home. Often Purpose Deficiency Syndrome sufferers feel their family values them only as a paycheck. Purpose Deficiency Syndrome often makes a homemaker feel like an "indentured servant." When Purpose Deficiency Syndrome reveals itself with these feelings, it becomes obvious that purpose deficiency exists at home. It is important to act now to prevent Purpose Deficiency Syndrome in your home life.

Discuss your purpose with your family. Lead your family through the character equation. Develop a purpose statement for your family that ties all the individual purposes of your family members together. Develop an icon as a symbol of your family's life purpose.

While vacationing on Lake Michigan, our family discussed the issue of purpose. While there I worked through the exercises in chapter 2. My wife Teri, and our kids—Lauren, Will, and Mary Grayson—worked through the exercise as well. Together we found the common foundation of our lives that has become our family's purpose. We agreed that our family's purpose is "building faith, family, and friendship." I identified with the statement so much that I adopted it as my personal purpose. Wherever Teri and I go, our purpose goes along to help us make good decisions. When Lauren, Will, and Mary Grayson are at parties with friends, our purpose is there to help them make good decisions. If a "friend" offers them a drink, they ask themselves, "Would drinking build my faith, my family, or my friendships?" I hope they conclude a friend would not tempt a young teenager to drink. Our purpose is not supported by the offer, and it is declined.

Aligning your life's purpose with the purpose of your work and the purpose of your family prevents Purpose Deficiency Syndrome from creeping in. If you want to realize your purpose in the future, you must focus on your purpose today.

LIFE IN THE FUTURE

Part of the motivation of understanding our purpose today is to ensure that we not look back at the end of our lives and wish we had lived differently. Solomon wrote, "Wealth is worthless in the day of wrath, but righteousness delivers from death" (Prov. 11:4). A life lived solely for the purpose of building a stable of cars, homes, vacations, and bank accounts will find those commodities do not satisfy on the last day of life. It is too late to begin thinking about your purpose on the last day of your life. So it is appropriate to test your purpose against the future, to think about your purpose today as if today were the last day of your life.

Given your purpose statement, imagine you and I are having dinner five years from now. You've had a hard day at work, and I say, "Tell me about your day." Respond as if it were today. Then assess your response to determine if your purpose statement is moving you in the right direction. For example, I might say: "I had a great day. Three new people started to work with us, and we immediately hit it off. A client remarked how well our work has helped their culture grow to be friendly and productive. I helped develop an impacting idea for another client. I really sense I am in the right place. Teri and I made plans for a weekend getaway, just the two of us. Lauren, Will, and Mary Grayson met me at the door with hugs and kisses. I had a great day."

Is this day possible if I focus on my purpose? Yes! Is the possibility of that day worth the sacrifice necessary to follow my purpose? The answer is a resounding yes.

Now it is your turn. Is your day possible, given your purpose? Is the possibility of that day compelling? If not, go back to step 1 and keep working until your purpose is clear.

THE POWER OF ALIGNMENT

Alignment is a principle we employ in many areas of life. We have the tires on a car aligned so the ride will be smooth and to extend the life of the tires. We have eyeglasses aligned with our ever-changing vision so we can see an image in sharp focus. Hanging a door on its frame requires alignment so the door will open and close smoothly. Aligning tires on cars, eyeglasses with eyes, and doors with their frames allows them to function as they are intended. Aligning our life with our life's purpose allows us to function as we are intended.

Your response to the questions on the previous page may have created a gulf between the place you are today and the place you want and need to be. You are adjusting and aligning your life to your purpose. This is a process you will repeat the rest of your life. Do not be discouraged because you have taken the first step necessary to realize your purpose. You have embarked on a lifelong journey of becoming a person of character.

GOLF IS LIFE

I saw a T-shirt bearing the message, "Golf is life!" While golf is not life to me, I do enjoy playing a few times each year. One day I was playing with a friend who is a club professional. We stepped on to the first tee, and I began lining up my shot. I picked a target, a tree about two hundred yards away in the middle of the fairway. Then I placed the ball on the tee and began a process of eyeing the tree then eyeing the ball. Tree. Ball. Tree. Ball. Tree. Ball. My eyes would gaze two hundred yards away then instantly to the ball at my feet. My friend grew frustrated with my novice technique and finally intervened. "What are you doing?" he exclaimed. Then he taught me a lesson about golf, and I learned a lesson about life.

He told me the target, the tree two hundred yards away, was the correct objective but that my technique would not result in my hitting the target. The tree was too far away to be accurately aligned with the ball. He pointed to a small piece of paper positioned about 75 yards down the fairway. He instructed me to align my ball with the paper and the paper with the tree. I formed a line using the three points—the ball, the paper, and the tree. Then my golf instructor taught me an important lesson about life. He said, "Once you have aligned your ball with the paper and the tree, focus on the paper and you will hit the tree." I did. It works.

APPLYING MY GOLF LESSON TO LIFE

That technique works in golf, and it works in life. The tee box represents where you are today, initiating the character-equation process. The piece of paper represents your roles and responsibilities at work and at home. The tree represents your life's purpose. The hole on the green is your vision.

The hole is often hidden from view when we are standing on the tee box. The scorecard is a picture of the green's position. Likewise, at the beginning of the character-equation process, it is often hard to see where our purpose may lead. That is why we paint a picture of how we will look and feel if we accomplish our purpose. That is our vision.

While it is in view, the tree is too far away to gauge perfectly the correct club, speed of the swing, and foot placement. That is why the piece of paper is so important. The piece of paper gives the golfer perspective about distance, and it provides a point for alignment with the tree. Likewise, our purpose (the tree) can seem too far away, too abstract. We know our abilities, passion, and relationships that combine to form our target, but we sometimes need more definition in order to take steps toward our purpose. Our roles and responsibilities (the piece of paper) give us the needed platform to live out our purpose today.

Applying my golf lesson to life, I learned that by focusing on my roles and responsibilities today (piece of paper) in a way that is consistent with my purpose I begin to understand and grow toward my purpose (the tree). As I gain a clearer perspective of my purpose, the vision (the hole on the green) suddenly appears achievable; and I am even more compelled to accomplish my purpose.

That is the power of alignment. Lining up all the areas of our life with our life's purpose allows us to function and become a person of true character.

THE MARK OF A PURPOSEFUL LIFE

Dietrich Bonhoeffer grew up in Germany in the years prior to World War II. Dietrich was a model German child, demonstrating the German passion for loyalty and service. He entered the ministry and was trained by the finest schools in Germany, England, and the United States.

While Dietrich was attending Union Theological Seminary in New York, Adolph Hitler assumed power in his homeland.[1] Though many of his friends in Germany told Dietrich of the horrible crimes committed by Hitler and the Third Reich, the loyal Dietrich dismissed their reports. In time the truth became undeniable. His loyalty to truth and his passion to serve others compelled him to move home.

Dietrich Bonhoeffer was a man of purpose. Though his actions were unpopular with the leaders of the state-sanctioned church, He opposed Hitler. Eventually, Dietrich was imprisoned. Just four days before the fall of Hitler, he was executed.

The life of Dietrich Bonhoeffer dramatically illustrates the mark of a purposeful life. Aligning your life to your purpose will always require sacrifice. Aligning your life to your purpose means you are sacrificing your agenda, ego, and desires in favor of your purpose.

LINKING PURPOSE AND PRACTICE

Paul called the living out of our purpose a "living sacrifice." He wrote, "Therefore, I urge you, brothers, in view of God's mercy, to offer your bodies as living sacrifices, holy and pleasing to God—this is your spiritual act of worship. Do not conform any longer to the pattern of this world, but be transformed by the renewing of your mind. Then you will be able to test and approve what God's will is—his good, pleasing and perfect will" (Rom. 12:1–2).

Paul linked our purpose in life to our practice of life. He taught that the more we conform to our purpose, the better we understand that purpose. Then the more we understand our purpose, the more we want to live in a way consistent with our purpose.

Surprisingly, we find that our "living sacrifices" are not sacrifices at all. Following an understood, aligned purpose requires what may appear to be a sacrifice but always results in fulfillment, stability, and meaning.

Relating our lives to Bonhoeffer-like sacrifice is difficult because few people will experience physical death due to the purposeful practice of life. The living sacrifice most of us are called to practice requires dying to our own desires.

Millard Fuller is a living example of purposeful practice. While attending the University of Alabama Law School, Fuller and a friend formed a marketing firm. Fuller's drive and business acumen made him a millionaire at age twenty-nine. But as his business prospered, his health and marriage suffered. Fuller reevaluated his purpose and direction. His soul-searching led to reconciliation with his wife and new direction for his life. The Fullers took an uncommon step: They sold all of their possessions and gave the money to the poor. Then with Clarence Jordan the Fullers began an effort to build affordable housing for low-income families. Today we know that nonprofit enterprise as Habitat for Humanity. Since its founding in 1976, Habitat for Humanity has built more than 70,000 homes providing more than 350,000 people with safe, respectable, and affordable shelter.[2] Millard Fuller presented his body as a "living sacrifice."

Practicing your purpose rarely results in physical death or in chunking a lucrative career for humanitarian causes. Practicing your purpose mostly results in a new understanding of and opportunity in everyday living. You may not be purposed to change your career like Fuller; you may be called to be right where you are. If so, understanding your purpose results in new energy, perseverance, and opportunity.

Mike Kolen's nickname is "Captain Crunch." Mike was given that name because of his hard hitting from the linebacker position for Auburn University and later for the Miami Dolphins. He was a rookie on the Dolphins team the first year Don Shula was head coach. From his first day with the Dolphins, Coach Shula communicated their purpose of winning the Super Bowl.

Coach Shula changed the offensive and defensive schemes of the team. Shula worked Mike and his teammates hard—harder than most of the guys had ever worked. Most teams may practice three times a day in the preseason. Shula practiced his team seven times a day. The Dolphins started work at 6 A.M. and after a number of breaks ended the day at 11 P.M.

Mike Kolen and the other guys practiced hard. The Dolphins were a purpose-driven team. The first year of Shula's rule the Dolphins made it to the Super Bowl and lost. The second year of Shula's tenure the Dolphins repeated in the Super Bowl, but this time they became world champions.

Did Mike Kolen and his teammates sacrifice by practicing from 6 A.M. to 11 P.M.? Yes, but ask them today, and their strongest memory is winning the Super Bowl. Mike wears his ring as evidence that his sacrifice turned to fulfillment, stability, and meaning as he and the Dolphins accomplished their purpose.

Dietrich Bonhoeffer's sacrifice turned to joy, even in prison, as he practiced his purpose. The way he lived was the result of the reason he lived. His purpose compelled his action, and his action reinforced his purpose. Millard Fuller found his purpose in a different line of work, so he traded the lucrative life he knew for the fulfillment, stability, and meaning of life aligned with his purpose.

THE CHARACTER EQUATION

The character equation links the purpose and practice of life. True character is the product of both purpose and practice. The next section of this book reveals the practice of a purposeful life. The ten practices are the "living sacrifices" the apostle Paul described as the way to understanding our purpose. All ten practices support the three elements of purpose, which are abilities, passion, and relationships. But each practice impacts one of the three elements of purpose more than the other two. Three of the practices support our abilities. These are balance, stewardship, and learning. Three of the practices support our passion. They are integrity, service, and promise keeping. The remaining four practices—expressed value, encouragement, communication, and accountability—support our relationships.

As you read, compare the practices with your life. How are you living in each area? What changes can you make to gain a better understanding of your purpose and build your character muscle?

APPLY THE CHARACTER EQUATION

1. Write your employer's purpose statement.
2. Write your own personal purpose statement.
3. List three ways you can fulfill your purpose while working to fulfill your employer's purpose.
4. What "living sacrifices" do you expect to make while practicing your purpose?
5. In what ways can you imagine your "living sacrifices" will turn to joy?

FOUR

$EV = Expressed\ Value$

MY DAY AT THE OFFICE

*L*eah had worked in our company for five years. During that time Leah seemed to go out of her way to make life difficult for her coworkers. A scowl adorned her face every morning. Breaks were a time for Leah to get away from her coworkers, but that was OK with everyone because of the hateful way she treated most of them.

When Leah entered the office one morning wearing a big grin, her coworkers were curious. Why the sudden change in her attitude? Some jokingly speculated Leah had a face-lift, and the procedure permanently fixed her face in the position of a smile. The reason for Leah's grin also provided an insight into the reason Leah wore a scowl for five years.

Leah had been married seven years, and most of that time she and her husband had tried to have children, but she was unable to get pregnant. The pain of her infertility manifested itself every day in the hateful way she interacted with others. Leah's grin was an announcement that a child was on the way.

For five years Leah's coworkers responded to her mean spirit in kind. For five years her coworkers made Leah the brunt of their jokes. Stories about Leah were circulated through the company grapevine. Her coworkers were quick to judge Leah but slow to help her. In fact, it took an incident on my most memorable day to bring Leah's coworkers to understand the practice of expressed value.

Leah's obstetrician asked for a special, short-term consideration based on medical necessity. The physician asked management to extend to Leah an extra break in the afternoon and to allow her to prop her feet up at her desk.

The request was granted, and Leah took her first extra break the same afternoon.

Leah had not returned from her extra break before five of her coworkers appeared at my door. These women were bent out of shape because of Leah's break. They reasoned: "If she gets an extra break, we should get an extra break. If we don't get the break, she should not have the break either." It did not matter to the women that Leah had a medical problem or that Leah had been easier to live with since becoming pregnant. In their minds this was payback time. Leah's coworkers took her medical misfortune and tried to hurt her when they should have been helping her. Purpose Deficiency Syndrome caused the women to miss the opportunity to show Leah how much they valued their relationship with her.

The word *value* often describes the end result of the corporate effort. "We are building value for our shareholders," a CEO might say. In this sense, the word *value* is a noun, but in the character equation the word *value* is a verb! Here value is a call to action; and if the call is answered, the CEO's desire for shareholder value will be satisfied.

In workplaces everywhere enormous amounts of time and productive energy are spent working out issues of pettiness and jealousy. Imagine the amount of time Leah's coworkers must have spent over the years tearing her down. Consider the ripple effect of their actions when others got caught up in the talk. The amount of lost productivity had to have been staggering. The women's Purpose Deficiency Syndrome caused them to devalue Leah, which led to a tangible loss of shareholder value.

What impact on shareholder value could the five women have had if they had chosen to value Leah? This circumstance was a great teacher. The women returned to their cubicles satisfied with Leah's extra break. Then they began to look for opportunities to show Leah they valued their relationship with her. Instead of gossiping about Leah, the women used their time for the benefit of the company which increased the quantity of their output. Expressing value to Leah naturally improved their self-images, and that improvement led to a higher quality work product. Their understanding of their personal purposes and the company's purpose increased as they built a relationship with Leah. The women contributed to an increase in shareholder value. Expressing value to those around us creates value for those around us.

PRACTICING VALUE CREATES VALUE FOR YOU

The practice of value is vital to the hope of realizing our purpose. Why? Because our purpose is rooted in relationship, and relationships flourish when value is expressed. Expressing value is the foundation of growing, healthy relationships.

Leah responded to her coworkers' expression of value in kind. Their relationship grew into friendship. The environment of their workplace improved. Leah and her coworkers solved a piece of the character equation and grew toward their purpose.

THE TWO SIDES OF VALUE

Almost every home and office has a ruler, the twelve-inch standard of measurement. Many rulers have two sides. On one side of the ruler, distance is measured in inches. The other side of the ruler measures distance according to the metric system. I am one of those people who have not yet committed the metric system to memory, so I use the side of the ruler that measures in inches. That side of the ruler comes natural to me. I understand distance measured by that side of the ruler, but sometimes I am required to measure distance using the metric system. I need to understand and use both sides of the ruler.

Value has two sides, the hard side and the soft side. As with the ruler, I need to understand and use both sides of value. In their book, *The Two Sides of Love*, John Trent and Gary Smalley contrast the two sides this way: "Hardside love is doing what's best for another person regardless of the cost. Held in balance, it's the ability to be consistent, to discipline, to protect, to challenge and to correct. Softside love is a tenderness that grows to be the same color as unconditional love. When held in balance, it manifests characteristics like compassion, sensitivity, patience and understanding."[1]

Just as you are endowed with inborn abilities and passion, you are endowed with a certain bent, a unique personality. Your personality naturally inclines you toward either the hard side or the soft side. I am naturally inclined toward the soft side but have learned and continue to develop my hard side. Understanding and balancing the two sides is essential if we hope to offer meaningful expressions of value that lead to long-standing relationships and ultimately our purpose.

THE SOFT SIDE OF VALUE

Expressions of soft-side value take the form of compassion, kindness, patience, long-suffering, trusting, and sensitivity. These qualities are most desirable but often not employed in a demanding, deadline-driven workplace environment. Circumstances all too often dictate our actions. Such was the case with Leah. Leah chose to allow her circumstance (infertility) to control her emotions. Leah's coworkers chose to allow their circumstance (an angry, hateful Leah) to dictate their actions toward her. Leah wanted and needed compassion while her coworkers wanted a peaceful working environment. Both Leah and the other women would have found satisfaction if they had taken the time to offer the soft side of value.

Sometimes expressing the soft side of value requires more than words. Compassion and long-suffering can bear a monetary cost. Consider this story:

> When police officer Phil Shultz found out last month that his three-year-old daughter had leukemia, he had to squeeze his limited time off from work to be with her. Thanks to fellow officers, time off is no longer a problem for the seven-year veteran of the force. He has at least 40 extra days coming to him.
>
> While Schultz and his wife, Amy, rotated nights at the hospital to be with daughter Lauren, he watched his vacation and compensatory time melt away. "I was beginning to wonder what I would do when I ran out," Schultz said. But his partners, led by officers Tom Schamerhorn and Steve Chaterton, would have nothing of it. Each officer donated four hours, and many have offered to give much more comp time, which they earn by working overtime. "We can't go out and cover the road for him," said Skip Beaver, director of staff services. "But there are things we can do. We wanted to make sure they knew we were here for them." "The day Lauren was diagnosed with leukemia, she was adopted by 100 people. They became like a second family for my whole family," Schultz said.[2]

When was the last time you "adopted" your coworker's family? Value can be expressed in response to a need. Value is received when the need is met. Soft-side value is what Leah, her coworkers, and the Schultz family needed. Soft-side value is the needs of people you face every day in the workplace, at home, and beyond.

THE HARD SIDE OF VALUE

I naturally understand I am valued when someone expresses value's soft side. Expressions from the other side, the hard side, are, for me, difficult to accept. I naturally respond to the soft-side approach, but I have learned the importance of the hard side.

Hard-side expressions of value include, among others, correcting, challenging, limiting options, disciplining, and loving confrontations about truth. Just as Leah needed the soft side of value, she also needed the hard side of value. Leah needed to understand how her difficult personality affected her coworkers. Though it was somewhat unnatural for me at the time, I called Leah in and confronted her in a loving way. I told her the truth about her actions. To my surprise she seemed relieved I had confronted her. She knew her actions had been inappropriate, and she took the opportunity of our discussion to talk about ways she could change her behavior.

Leah's coworkers needed the hard side of value as well. During their visit to my office, I challenged their thinking about Leah. I asked them what each would want me to do if they were in Leah's shoes. With that point etched clearly in their minds, the women retreated to their cubicles with a refreshed attitude.

The hard side of value is the picture of the mother eagle kicking her eaglet out of the nest and forcing it to fly. Her action is necessary for her child to live. Sometimes the same action is necessary in workplaces. I have concluded that hiring is more art than science. People are regularly placed in jobs for which they have little aptitude. In most cases the time comes for that person to move on, but often the person most affected by such a move is the last to know.

While consulting a company, I discovered a pattern to how people left their employment. It seemed the CEO of this organization was naturally inclined toward the soft side. He was so soft sided that tough issues rarely, if ever, were confronted. When it became obvious an employee was in the wrong job, this CEO would tell the others in the office he was going to let the employee go. A day would pass, then a week. Soon a month went by, and the person was still there. In time the affected employee would hear through the grapevine that his job was in jeopardy, or the employee would find some tangible evidence that his employment was over. In one case the employee was caught totally off guard when the new office phone directory was issued without her name in it and with another person bearing her title! The CEO could have made a positive difference in this young woman's life by balancing his soft side by doing the hard side's often hard job of simply telling the truth.

THE IMPORTANCE OF PURPOSE IN PRACTICE

During the 1997 Professional Golfers Association tournament at the Winged Foot Country Club, professional Ken Venturi was asked the question, "Why do you (PGA members) talk so much about the PGA as a family?" This was Venturi's response: "You learn from your parents those things you bring to the game like compassion, discipline, and honesty. You come out here and compete to win, but in the end the attitude is 'What can I do to help?'"

Expressing value, both the soft side and the hard side, builds relationships that grow into friendships and perhaps eventually even family. Relationships are a key to understanding our purpose, and yet our purpose keeps us focused on the importance of relationships. Our purpose causes us to ask the risky question, "What can I do to help?" Our purpose compels us to respond to a request by meeting the need even when doing so requires that we express value through the unnatural and uncomfortable side of value.

In his book *The Book of Virtues*, Bill Bennett wrote, "The demands of friendship—for frankness, for self-revelation, for taking friends' criticism as seriously as their expressions of admiration or praise, for stand-by-me loyalty, and for assistance to the point of self-sacrifice—are all potent encouragements to moral maturation and even ennoblement."[3]

Bennett gets it. He made the connection between our relationships and our character by pointing out the practices of value necessary for their development. Linking our purpose and our relationships produces friends and family. Our friends and family are those who stick with us through adversity, who give more often than they receive, and who encourage us to an ever-growing practice of life that results in the realization of our purpose.

APPLY THE CHARACTER EQUATION

1. Think about the people in your work world. Create a mental list starting at the top with the people you love the most. Next, begin scrolling down the list toward those people who are not your most favorite lunch buddies. Keep going down the list. Eventually you will hit rock bottom. You have found the person you love the least. Hold that person's image in your mind's eye.

2. How can you express value to the person you love the least? Avoid an answer such as "be nicer." Be specific such as asking the person to go on break or inquiring about his or her family.

3. Consider this question, If I were to leave my workplace to take another job, what would my coworkers, employer, or employees miss?

FIVE

$\mathscr{E}$ = Encouragement

MY DAY AT THE OFFICE

*M*arcia had worked in the financial industry for years. She had lived through the banking industry's cycles of consolidation before, but her experience did not seem to matter the morning of that unforgettable day. Marcia had talked with a friend who worked in a competing organization who passed along a rumor suggesting that our company was on the auction block. Marcia freaked!

The uncertainty of this possible change caused a crisis that paralyzed Marcia. She assumed her circumstances would take a turn for the worse. Perhaps she would lose her job. Maybe she would be reassigned to a new, unfamiliar area. The more Marcia thought about the rumor, the more plausible it seemed. Soon what was only a rumor became fact in her mind, sending her level of stress and fear through the roof.

THE NEED FOR ENCOURAGEMENT

Marcia's experience is typical of the Purpose Deficiency Syndrome sufferer. Living without an understood, stated purpose leaves the Purpose Deficiency Syndrome victim with no hope of rising above life's difficult circumstances. Many people with Purpose Deficiency Syndrome crawl into the dark deep hole of depression. Purpose Deficiency Syndrome can affect the individual physically. When the individual is affected physically, it affects the workplace. A recent projection suggests the cost of depressive disorders in the American workplace exceeds $40 billion. Absenteeism alone accounted for about 30 percent of the cost. Other factors in the total cost include losses arising from lower productivity, safety risks, accidents, suicide, and the cost of inadequate or inappropriate treatment for depression.[1]

Most workplaces operate on the philosophy that it does not matter how employees feel as long as they get the work done. Managers set unrealistic goals without considering the emotional impact of their employees' perceived failure. Coworkers participate in water cooler talk without concern for another's feelings. Someone starts or perpetuates a rumor about the future of a mortgage company, never pausing to consider how such talk might frighten someone like Marcia.

Emotion does matter, especially to those with Purpose Deficiency Syndrome. As Purpose Deficiency Syndrome victims wander through life, their emotions are blown around like a leaf in a tornado. With no sense of the future to offer balance, current circumstances dictate emotions. An unproductive response to crisis is often the result.

President John Kennedy said, "When written in Chinese, the word *crisis* is composed of two characters. One represents danger and the other represents opportunity."[2] Emotion influences our response to crisis. The Purpose Deficiency Syndrome sufferer often sees danger in a crisis while the purposeful often see opportunity. Marcia envisioned trouble while others heard the rumor and saw the possibility of an even brighter future.

Emotions rub off on others. Marcia's emotions about the rumored merger influenced another manager. Soon entire departments were caught up in the talk of gloom and doom. Marcia's case of Purpose Deficiency Syndrome was spreading.

Crisis comes in many forms, but always at the center is the issue of change. Usually without warning change takes its toll. The phone rings, and the message is the untimely death of a loved one. Perhaps the call is from your broker reporting the stock market is off four hundred points and the value of your once-flourishing portfolio is dropping like a rock. Maybe you have experienced the nausea of being summoned to the boss's office knowing your time with the company is about to end. Changes often lead to crisis.

Sometimes change can be a friend. Suppose your spending habits are out of control. Changing your purchasing pattern can lower your debt. If the state police honor you with a citation for speedy driving, changing your ground speed might save your insurance, perhaps your life. Technology is changing at a phenomenal rate and offering the opportunity for increased productivity. Achieving higher levels of productivity is the result of staying current with technological advances, and that requires change. Change is sometimes a friend, but our failure to embrace it leads to destruction.

Encouragement is a practice that helps navigate the crisis of change. Importantly, encouragement is the piece of the character equation that refreshes the emotion of the Purpose Deficiency Syndrome victim. Encouragement refreshes the purposeful as well with a call to continue living at a higher level.

I am reminded of the need for encouragement every year as the season changes from spring to summer. Summers are hot and humid in the South where I live. Temperatures can top out over 100° with humidity in the range of 90 percent or more. That is hot! So hot that I begin perspiring during the thirty-foot walk from my office door to my car. On those rare occasions when Teri entices me outside for a few hours of yard work, my throat feels as dry as Main Street on *Gunsmoke*. At just the right time, Lauren shows up with a tall glass of ice water, and I quickly drench my parched throat. That is refreshment! That is encouragement!

Encouraging Acts

Impulsive Encouragement

Marcia surprised me on that unforgettable day. I had not prepared to meet with her, but suddenly I was in the midst of an impromptu meeting with a manager whose throat was parched dry from her crisis. Marcia needed the cool refreshment of encouragement. I encouraged Marcia with the reassuring words that a merger was not in the works.

My encouragement was impromptu, impulsive. Impulsive encouragement occurs every day. You step on the elevator after a meeting and offer an encouraging word to another person. You did not plan to offer your words, but you took advantage of the opportunity. Impulsive encouragement occurs when you happen to see a card that reminds you of a friend and you send it. I had not planned to encourage Marcia that day, but the experience taught me an important lesson. I encouraged Marcia by revealing that the rumor was false, rendering the circumstance of the merger to be benign. Marcia exited my office sure to return when the next rumor became her crisis. What if I had encouraged Marcia by leading her to understand her purpose regardless of the circumstance? I learned intentional encouragement is much more effective than impulsive encouragement.

Intentional Encouragement

Intentional encouragement is planned. The intentional encourager thinks about his or her purpose every day. The intentional encourager looks for ways to help others solve the character equation and enjoy significance, peace, and contentment.

Some years ago Al Rhodes and Clyde Upchurch, two Atlanta business-men, attended a convention in Toronto. Though competitors, Al and Clyde did not know each other until one night during the convention when Al noticed a man standing alone. Al made his way over and met Clyde for the first time. After the normal exchange of names, Al asked Clyde where he lived. "Atlanta, Georgia," replied Clyde. The pair were delighted to find their hometown in common.

"What part of Atlanta?" Clyde asked.

Al announced, "Marietta."

"So do I," Clyde said, smiling in disbelief.

Al pressed the issue, "What area of Marietta?"

These competitors had each traveled to Toronto and found that not only were they in the same business competing for many of the same accounts in the same city but they also lived just one block from each other.

When they returned to Atlanta, Al invited Clyde to join the FCCI, a fellowship of business owners.[3] Clyde did not take the invitation lightly. After all, how often does your principal competitor invite you into a group where he has substantial business relationships? Those invitations are rare, but Al and Clyde's experience is a great picture of intentional encouragement.

The intentional encourager has at least four characteristics. They are:

1. Confidence of purpose
2. Willingness to risk reputation
3. Commitment to communicate the importance of another's future
4. Ability to compel others into action

1. CONFIDENCE OF PURPOSE

Why would Al Rhodes introduce his competitor to potential clients? Especially some of Al's own clients? The reason is simple. Al knows his purpose in life is more important than any competitor or any client. Success in life is achieving your purpose. So Al practiced encouragement in Clyde's life as part of the fulfillment of his purpose. Al never considered the possible loss of business to Clyde.

Confidence in your purpose creates the flexibility to do the uncommon such as encouraging your competitor. Such confidence causes you to look beyond today's logical decision to the possibility offered by your purpose. Logic demanded Al's quick exit in Toronto after meeting Clyde. Logic said: "This is your competitor. Smile. Shake his hand, then get out of here." Purpose said, "Trust me," and that is exactly what Al did.

Marcia, suffering from Purpose Deficiency Syndrome, had no purpose in which to trust. Thus, her only hope was in what can be seen, her circumstances. That explains her knee-jerk reaction to the merger rumor. A first step of being an intentional encourager in people's lives is to help them discover their purpose.

2. WILLINGNESS TO RISK REPUTATION

Did Al really know Clyde when he proposed Clyde for membership in FCCI? They had been aquatinted for only a short time. Al took a risk with Clyde. In time Clyde could have proven his interest in FCCI was purely to obtain new business. Clyde could have embarrassed Al by not paying his dues timely. Al also risked his peers thinking he had lost his mind by inviting his competitor. Fortunately Clyde proved to be a man of character, just as Al thought. And Al's peers, what did they think of Al's action of intentional encouragement? Many followed Al's example by inviting their competitors. Secure in his purpose, Al risked his own reputation to encourage Clyde.

When people's purpose is not known, they shy away from taking risks. If Marcia had been a purposeful person at the time of the rumor, she would have confidently risked her reputation by declaring the opportunity presented by the proposed corporate marriage. Her Purpose Deficiency Syndrome-ridden coworkers may have scoffed at her optimism, but Marcia would have continued encouraging them. The second step of being an intentional encourager is to demonstrate your confidence of purpose by risking your reputation to follow that purpose. Your action compels others to trust their purpose.

3. COMMITMENT TO COMMUNICATE THE IMPORTANCE OF ANOTHER'S FUTURE

Al and Clyde have lived through a number of business cycles. Both have had good years, and both have had disappointing years. Through it all Al and Clyde have supported each other by this important third step of intentional encouragement. When one of the men is down, the other comes around to help maintain focus on the purpose.

Everyone spends time in the forest of confusion. This is the place where you "cannot see the forest for the trees." It is there that the intentional encourager offers words of a bright future. "Think about all the people you will impact by staying focused on your purpose" is something an encourager may tell a friend.

That was the message Marcia needed on that unforgettable day. I had the perfect opportunity to show Marcia where to find the refreshment of encouragement for herself. Instead, I impulsively handed her a cool glass of encouragement. I simply told her the crisis had been averted. If I had been an intentional encourager at the time, I would have helped her find her purpose. By offering a soothing word, I created her dependence on me. Communicating words of a bright future creates dependence on the purpose.

4. ABILITY TO COMPEL OTHERS INTO ACTION

Al Rhodes is an uncommon man. His uncommon acts of intentional encouragement have helped Clyde understand his purpose. Today, both men are intentional encouragers. These competitors have combined parties for the employees of both companies. Both men are helping their employees understand purpose and learn to put it into practice. Each challenges the others to practice a purposeful life. The fourth step of intentional encouragement is helping others find ways to practice their purpose.

THE IMPORTANCE OF PURPOSE IN PRACTICE

Encouragement is the practice that refreshes others' emotions, enabling them to live out their purpose. Interestingly, the encourager is refreshed along with the encouraged. Solomon said, "A generous man will prosper; he who refreshes others will himself be refreshed" (Prov. 11:25). In other words, the more we encourage others, the more encouraged we become. That is important in the character equation because it is the person of character who so often is the encourager. Expended energy to encourage another person is not wasted; it is investment that yields results in both the life of the encouraged and the life of the encourager.

Marcia continued to show up at my door when circumstances turned to crisis. Eventually, Marcia solved the character equation and arrested her Purpose Deficiency Syndrome. Today, she too is an intentional encourager. What about you?

APPLY THE CHARACTER EQUATION

1. How do you wish others would treat you when you need encouragement?
2. In what ways do you encourage others?
3. On a scale of 1 to 5, 5 being most confident, rate your level of confidence in your understanding of your purpose. If your response is between 1 and 3, invest time in working through purpose again in chapter 3.
4. When was the last time you risked your reputation? Who in your workplace could you encourage in this way?

SIX

$\mathcal{L}$ = Learning

MY DAY AT THE OFFICE

*A*ubrey, our internal auditor, dropped in and disclosed the existence of a consistent, repetitive error in our computer system. The cost to fix the failure was potentially in the millions of dollars.

Problems rarely get better with age, so I hopped up from the desk and made my way down to the department responsible for the error. "We have a problem, folks," I said. Everyone's attention turned to me. Brainstorming the possible causes of the problem led us to review the files containing the error. Suddenly a common thread emerged in all the files. That common thread was Mike. Mike had input all of the errors.

The tension was thick. All eyes seemed to turn and fix on the culprit of the problem. The look on Mike's face screamed embarrassment and cried for help. Mike and I returned to my office. The walk seemed longer than usual. Mike felt as if he were being led from death row to the electric chair, and I was thinking about flipping the switch!

"What in the heck happened, Mike?" was my not-so-gentle opening salvo. His response was unexpected. "Well, I have been working here about six months. In that short period of time, I have seen a half dozen or more people fired on the spot for making a single mistake. I am a single parent, and I need this job. I was unsure of what I was doing, but I felt that even asking a question would put me at risk of losing my job. So I did not ask any questions and just hoped I was getting it right. Looking back now, I would rather have lost my job for asking questions than to lose it under these circumstances."

I left Mike in my office and visited our personnel director. The personnel director told me Mike's supervisor was notorious for firing people. While not dismissing Mike's responsibility for his own actions, the personnel director confirmed his assertion that the department's culture is dominated by fear.

THE NEED TO LEARN

Repetitive error is a failure to learn and a sign of Purpose Deficiency Syndrome. Mike certainly made a bushel of repetitive errors. But Mike was not the only person with a learning disability. Mike's supervisor was afflicted as well. The supervisor repeatedly failed to learn the problems created by a culture where people are afraid to ask questions.

Purpose Deficiency Syndrome causes its victims to aim low in life. Aiming low leaves the Purpose Deficiency Syndrome sufferer with the impression that life cannot really improve from its current point. Purpose Deficiency Syndrome sufferers feel they have arrived at the pinnacle of all they can achieve. Self-preservation becomes essential. That was the supervisor's problem. She did not see a greater purpose in her work, so she hunkered down. She dug in and dared anyone to make an error because she feared errors might topple her from her pinnacle to which she could never return.

People with Purpose Deficiency Syndrome often do not care about anything other than themselves. That was Mike. Mike wrapped his failure in the noble cloak of providing for his child. While I am sensitive to the difficulty of single parenting, in time I knew Mike's reasoning was simply a façade. Purpose Deficiency Syndrome and its cynical "whatever" attitude hardened Mike. He came to work each day doing just enough to get by and not caring about the quality of his work. Since Mike's life was not routed to a higher purpose, he was not interested in learning from his and other people's errors.

People of character are focused on their purpose. They see a wide gulf between their current place in life and the ultimate fulfillment of their purpose. The gulf is not discouraging to the purposeful people of character, because they know it is their practice of life that will bring them closer to their purpose. That is the application of the character equation.

People who are daily solving the character equation are constantly challenging their own practice of life. They are looking for new ways, better ways to live. They attack mundane work projects and anticipate a breakthrough. These are the people who come up with innovative ideas and creative solutions.

Students of the character equation have the ideas and the solutions because they accept as fact that mistakes and errors are teachers, not executioners. These people make a mistake, then quickly dissect it, learn from it, make the necessary changes, put it behind them, and as a result grow toward their purpose.

Students applying the character equation are the 20 percent responding as "active" in the Wilson Learning study.[1] These are the people who learn and grow. When someone in the other 80 percent makes it into the ranks of management, Purpose Deficiency Syndrome can become institutionalized and spread throughout the workplace. Robert McMath, in his book *What Were They Thinking?* writes, "We've created a management environment that rewards people for constructing facades and ignoring reality."[2] That was certainly true of Mike's department. His supervisor was more concerned with perception than she was with reality. The results could have been disastrous.

What if Thomas Edison had "constructed a facade" for his friends? What if he had been more concerned with appearances than he was with reality? Edison could have put more emphasis on what others thought about him than he put on fulfilling his purpose. If he had, you would be reading this book by candlelight. Edison made more than ten thousand errors before the lightbulb worked. He used his mistakes as a platform for learning and ultimately fulfilled his purpose. Edison learned to learn.

LEARNING TO LEARN

Attention Deficit Disorder (ADD) seems to be a common disease among children. A medicine known as Ritalin helps the ADD victims overcome one of the main symptoms of the disease, which is an inability to focus. Children with ADD are easily distracted.

Purpose Deficiency Syndrome affects adults in much the same way. Void of purpose, we wander from one fad to the next. Without purpose we become distracted by the accomplishments and accumulation of those around us. Our distraction from our true purpose in life leads us to adopt the life and lifestyle of our friends and colleagues. When that life and that lifestyle do not satisfy our souls, we "construct a facade" to appear happy and together. Purpose Deficiency Syndrome is in control, leading its victim to an even lower point. It is here, behind the facade, that our rational thinking is replaced by a lie that suggests we must be perfect and error-free if we hope to find happiness or at least maintain the appearance of happiness.

Learning is to Purpose Deficiency Syndrome as Ritalin is to ADD. Learning is the catalyst for maintaining focus on our purpose. Learning sees error as the natural progression toward purpose. Instead of error distracting us from our purpose, learning uses our error as a stepping-stone to a better life.

Three steps are necessary for learning. They are:
1. Seeking significance instead of settling for success
2. Redefining failure and acknowledging error
3. Rebuilding and restoring

SEEKING SIGNIFICANCE INSTEAD OF SETTLING FOR SUCCESS

Success is a much-used term that defines what other people value. We are successful in someone's eyes if we make a certain amount of money, but the amount necessary for success is in the eye of the beholder. We are deemed successful if we get the promotion, but of course the job considered successful is in the eye of the beholder. Fame is considered a mark of success, but only if we are famous in the eye of the beholder. I sat next to a movie star while flying from Los Angeles to Atlanta. While a few people on the flight recognized him, I did not and had never heard of him. He was famous and successful in the eyes of a few but not in mine.

Mike's supervisor was preoccupied with success, which led her to do whatever was necessary to impress her colleagues. This included creating the impression of zero errors. Success, like beauty, is in the eye of the beholder, the other person. Living for success necessarily means we strive to measure up to another person's standard. Pursuing success on someone else's terms can compel us to construct the facade that inhibits learning.

Significance is a different achievement. Significance is the realization of our purpose. Because our purpose includes relationships, significance recognizes our contribution in another person's life, but that person does not define our significance. Significance is defined by our purpose.

Success inhibits learning because its pursuit can cause us to cover our errors. Significance, on the other hand, sees the potential to learn and grow from the error. Significance is more concerned with realizing our purpose than it is concerned with meeting another person's definition of success.

REDEFINING FAILURE AND ACKNOWLEDGING ERROR

Mike's supervisor treated a single error as a failure, and as McMath pointed out, his supervisor shared that perspective with many if not most managers. If we are to grow beyond our errors and realize the significance of our purpose, we must redefine *failure*. I believe failure is the unwillingness to learn.

Perhaps pride causes us to fail to learn from our errors. Many people are not willing to admit an error if the admission means falling short of someone's definition of *success*. Maybe fear of the consequences causes us to bury the mistake. Mike's errors were due, in part, to his fear of being fired. Both explanations are classic symptoms of Purpose Deficiency Syndrome and are overcome only when we humbly admit our mistakes, learn from them, and grow. Our unwillingness to acknowledge our errors is our true failure.

REBUILDING AND RESTORING

Our errors in life often hurt other people. Realizing our purpose is possible, even when we have hurt others, if we seek to rebuild and restore our relationships.

Rebuilding and restoring requires that we be approachable. When Purpose Deficiency Syndrome leads to the construction of a facade, we are not approachable. The trouble in Mike's department started long before he was hired. His trouble started when his supervisor constructed a facade. Orit Gadiesh, chairman of Bain & Company, speaks from years of experience consulting many companies, "Trouble starts when people are afraid to talk to the boss and ideas don't reach the top."[3] Ideas, errors, and other information that is stymied by an unapproachable facade is trouble for any organization, and it is trouble for any relationship.

Approachability is necessary to the process of rebuilding and restoring. The day I was informed of Mike's error was a difficult day. By the time the news of this problem reached me, I was worn out and irritable. My first impulse was to fly down to Mike's department and devour the error-maker. Fortunately, that still small voice in my soul reminded me to take a moment and regain my composure. This problem, as with all problems, could only be solved by reasonable, cool heads. The prophet Isaiah wrote, "Come . . . let us reason together" (Isa. 1:18). So I pulled a blank sheet of paper out and poured out my feelings, which were not very pleasant. With my anger now transferred to the paper, I simply wadded it up and tossed it in the trash. Dealing with errors is not always that simple, but I have found the process of writing out my feelings, especially when my feelings involve anger, to be therapeutic and to enhance my approachability.

Rebuilding and restoring will always require that we forgive ourselves, forgive others, and accept forgiveness from others. It is difficult to step from behind the facade and ask someone for forgiveness, but it is a necessary step if we desire relationships that lead to our purpose. John wrote, "If we confess our sins, he is faithful and just and will forgive us our sins and purify us from all unrighteousness" (1 John 1:9). Sometimes our errors are against God, and we need to ask for his forgiveness, but this biblical principle applies to our relationships as well. Forgiveness keeps our relationships pure and purposeful.

Forgiveness has been proven to offer the additional benefit of good health. A study published in the *Journal of Moral Education* found that "forgiveness was associated with positive psychological outcomes: reduced anxiety and depression and higher self-esteem."[4]

Finally, rebuilding and restoring requires that we put the error in the past. But errors bring consequences, and if we are the error-maker, that means we must take our lumps and move on.

Mark Gagnon worked as a clerk in the North Hampton, Massachusetts, store owned by James Brazeau. Brazeau had promised to bring Gagnon a New England Patriots hat when he returned from the game. Brazeau arrived as promised, hat in hand, only to discover Gagnon had stolen $4,382 worth of lottery tickets from the store. Gagnon was prosecuted, and just before he was sentenced, his former boss Brazeau walked over to the defendant's table and presented Gagnon with a paper bag and said, "I want this to be a learning experience for you."[5] The Patriots hat was inside the bag. The judge, watching from the bench, made the hat part of Gagnon's sentence, ordering Gagnon to wear the hat every time he ventured out into public for the next two years. Brazeau wanted to rebuild and restore the relationship with Gagnon. Giving Gagnon the hat said we can learn from this and move on.

THE IMPORTANCE OF PURPOSE IN PRACTICE

Learning is the catalyst for maintaining focus on our purpose. Learning is vital in the character equation because all people will err in the practice of life. How we respond to our error will help determine the character of the person we become. Humbly acknowledging our error, seeking and offering forgiveness, and rebuilding relationships leads to a greater understanding of our purpose. Covering over our error can lead to problems such as arrogance, pride, and hardheartedness, which are symptomatic of Purpose Deficiency Syndrome. If you are suffering with these symptoms of Purpose Deficiency Syndrome, take Ethyl Barrymore's advice, "It's what you learn after you know it all that counts."

APPLY THE CHARACTER EQUATION

1. Consider a recent error or mistake you made. Is the error familiar? Have you made this mistake before, maybe more than once? Has the

error become repetitive? If so, what changes do you need to make? Who was involved in the error that needs your forgiveness, or whose forgiveness do you need?

2. Define *success*. What relevance does this definition have to your purpose? What changes are needed to your definition to move the meaning from success to significance?

SEVEN

$\mathcal{B} = \mathcal{B}alance$

MY DAY AT THE OFFICE

*C*laire did the best she could. She tried to juggle a dozen different balls at the same time. Finally, her hands just gave out. That is when I was called. Claire unconsciously ran her hand too far into the document feeder, and the machine grabbed it. The pain of the accident caused Claire to collapse. The paramedics transported her to the hospital.

The events of the day forced Claire to stop and reflect on her life. Later that evening, stretched out on her hospital bed, Claire likened her life to that of a juggler. She described all the balls she was juggling. Of course, I was aware of her work responsibilities. Away from the office two of Claire's three children were each playing soccer and baseball. Her third child was taking piano and gymnastics. She was a member of the church choir and volunteered with the Red Cross. Keeping her home together and making time to be with her husband who traveled frequently were priorities, too.

CLAIRE'S DAY

BZZZZZZZ! Get up! Make breakfast for everyone, get the kids ready for school, make lunches, get the kids to school, get herself dressed, and get all this done and arrive at work by 8 A.M. Work all day. Get the kids. Take Tommy to soccer practice, Emily to piano across town, James to baseball. Run home, change clothes, straighten up the house, drive through McDonalds, pick up Tommy from soccer and drive him to baseball while he eats and changes clothes in the backseat. Pick up James from baseball and drive him to soccer while he eats and changes clothes in the backseat. Drop James, enjoy the quiet while contemplating how James's and Tommy's practice schedules could have worked out worse. Pick up Emily and feed her on the return trips to get the boys, ever thankful her gymnastics workout is tomorrow night. Pick up boys. Discuss homework. Baths and in bed. Talk to husband who is in another city. Sleep. Get up and start again.

From the perspective of the hospital bed, Claire could see why her brain shut down and why the result was a painful accident. Claire was worn out physically. The stress of trying to keep all the balls in the air had depleted her emotionally as well. Interestingly, though Claire was very active, she felt that she was not accomplishing anything of value.

THE NEED FOR BALANCE

Many people share Claire's predicament. Radio, television, infomercials, books, and "here today, gone tomorrow" gurus tell us we can have it all. Believing their advice, we indulge and indulge and indulge. Then one day, like Claire, we crash and ask why. The answer is usually the same. Our life is out of balance. "Having it all" as defined by the television pitchman is a myth. Believing we are somehow different from Claire, most of us pursue this dream anyway. In hindsight the stress of a life out of balance is predictable.

These high levels of imbalance-related stresses are occurring in a time when people, according to the U.S. Department of Labor statistics, are working less—less, in fact, than the hours our parents and grandparents worked. In 1948, the average number of hours worked per week was 42.8. In 1998, the average person worked 39.5 hours per week.[1]

But are we really working fewer hours? The Labor Department does not measure the time Claire spends each day conducting business with her cell phone while transporting her kids to sports practices. The Labor Department statistic does not include the time invested late at night checking E-mail. Michael Abiodun, a chemist, says, "It seems like you work, work, work. I take my work with me when I'm going home. If I can't get the project done during the day, I think about it."[2]

Perhaps the great advances in technology we enjoy are actually contributing to the imbalance many people are facing. Cell phones are in our cars, our purses, and our pockets. Pagers can find us at thirty thousand feet aboard any aircraft anywhere in the world. Laptops keep us connected to the Internet and E-mail. Voice mail has enhanced the game of phone tag. All of these technological advances are great, but they have created an environment where we cannot get away from work. Pressing the off button on our phone or pager often breeds guilt. Leaving the laptop at home during a family trip gives its owner a naked feeling.

Work is the traditional culprit of those living an unbalanced life, and for many people the demands of work can be an obstacle to a balanced life. But for many others the lack of balance is due to other factors, ranging from working too little to trying to conquer every avenue life offers, just like Claire. An unbalanced life manifests itself in these ways, but the origin of the imbalance is found much deeper than what we see.

The root problem of a life marked by imbalance is Purpose Deficiency Syndrome. Why do people try to "have it all" by conquering every avenue of life? Because people who have lost their balance have allowed the television pitchman to define what "having it all" means. Purpose Deficiency Syndrome numbs the soul, the place where our purpose resides, until we are flat on our backs in a hospital bed.

The balanced person understands that "having it all" means they accomplish their purpose. The balanced person is content in the pursuit of his or her purpose.

THREE STEPS TO BALANCE

1. GET ORGANIZED AROUND YOUR PURPOSE

Your purpose statement is truly the organizing principle of your life. The answers to many practical questions you face every day can be found in this simple, concise statement, if you follow it. That is a big if! We tend to work through the painstaking process of understanding our purpose, then return to our old pattern of living.

Ask most people today, "What are your priorities?" and they will pull out a legal-pad-size list. Most of us would identify not one but many priorities in life. Bill Pollard, chairman of the board of ServiceMaster, was asked by a young executive, "Mr. Pollard, I have a job with a lot of responsibility. I have responsibility at church and in the community. I am married, and we have three children. How can I manage all I have to do?" In other words, the young executive was asking how he could live a balanced life in the face of so many demands, responsibilities, and activities. Mr. Pollard responded, "The word *priority* was not used in its plural form until this century." The concept of multiple priorities in life, according to Mr. Pollard, is a recent phenomenon. Perhaps this is the answer to the young man's question. Balance is possible if we practice life according to a single priority, and that single priority is our purpose.

We lose our balance because we are attempting to carry jobs, debt, relationships, and activities that have no relation to our purpose and for which we are not equipped. Sometimes it takes a Claire-like crash to wake us up to the reality that finding balance is an act of the will to practice our purpose in every area of life.

The Merck Family Fund commissioned a poll that revealed an interesting trend in America. From 1990 to 1995, "nearly one-third of us voluntarily changed the way we live and work because of new priorities. These people simplified their lives in order to be closer to their families, to do more satisfying work and volunteering, and to escape the pressure-filled life of acquisition."[3] These people, seeking balance, stepped out of the rat race and reassessed their list of priorities. Many people concluded there is only one priority in life—your purpose.

Susan Gregory, author of *Out of the Rat Race,* wrote: "Simplicity is much more than cutting back on time- and money-grabbing activities. Simple living isn't back-to-the-land or turning back the hands of time. It's not cheap living or living without involvement in many activities. Rather, simple living is understanding intimately about who we are as individuals, going deep into ourselves and learning what makes us tick."[4] The simplicity about which Gregory wrote is balance, and balance is found by organizing your life around your purpose. Simple to say, difficult to do consistently. Think of your purpose as a pair of eyeglasses. Everything you see should be filtered through the lens of your purpose. Every activity, job, cause, and relationship should be filtered through the lens of your purpose.

2. DEFINE THE DIMENSIONS OF YOUR LIFE

Finding balance in life is a big job. It can be a daunting task. Big, daunting jobs can be simplified by breaking the task into smaller parts. The task of finding balance is simplified when our life is broken down into these four dimensions: intellectual, physical, spiritual, and social.

Intellectual

The intellectual dimension of our lives includes all those activities designed to stimulate our ability to think. Work is part of this dimension as well as time spent reading and researching topics of interest. A balanced life emphasizes the intellectual dimension in the context of purpose. I am called to build people. That is my purpose. So what do I say when a lucrative, work-related opportunity unrelated to my purpose comes my way? Thanks, but no thanks? Why? Because I know I am uniquely equipped to accomplish my purpose; and it is my purpose that brings contentment, significance, and peace. Unfortunately, I was not born understanding this principle. I learned it the hard way. Experience has taught me that straying from my purpose results in imbalance.

Physical

Are you physically fit? That is the bottom line. Exercise, rest, and diet are the heart of the issue. Too many people underemphasize this dimension. A study by Ohio University and Scripps Howard News Service found that more than 75 percent of Americans are overweight, and approximately 25 percent of Americans are obese. Tom McMillan, cochairman of the President's Council on Physical Fitness, said, "We've become a spectator nation. We are happy to watch the million dollar athlete on television, but we don't want to do anything ourselves."[5] If you are huffing and puffing after an evening of watching Monday night football, this dimension needs your attention.

We can overemphasize our physical dimension also. Our desire for good health can become a vain pursuit. We run, lift weights, diet, crunch our tummies, and hang by our toes, sculpting our bodies for the viewing public. Instead, exercise to train and condition your body for the race of life. If you are spending more time at the gym or spa than you are at home, recalibrate your practice into alignment with your purpose.

Spiritual

Claire was not initially thankful for her injury and unexpected overnight visit to the hospital. Soon she learned an important truth: Lying flat on your back in a hospital bed can be a blessing. When lying flat on your back, your eyes naturally look up. When flattened by life's unexpected injuries, our perspective about life can "look up" as well.

Claire asked a lot of questions about her life. Big questions. Questions like, What if my accident were fatal? Where would I be now? Why am I here? Who put me here? Claire is fortunate the accident was serious enough to cause her to think about these issues. Claire is also fortunate that her accident was not fatal because now she has a second chance to consider life's biggest questions.

James Dobson said, "When you come to the end of your life, the only thing that will matter is who you loved, who loved you, and what you did for your Creator."[6] A balanced person asks life's biggest questions and finds the answers before she is lying flat on her deathbed. Asking and answering these questions is essential to living a purposeful life.

Social

The character equation emphasizes relationships. Abilities and passion are summed then multiplied by relationships. Relationships in the character equation answer the question, For whom is my purpose intended? Practicing balance in life requires that we continually ask: "Am I involved in a meaningful way with the people for whom my purpose is intended? How am I sharing my life with the people for whom my purpose is intended?"

While personality influences our social dimension toward or away from interaction with others, we are all built for fellowship. Teri, my wife, and I are good examples of two people with two different appetites for social interaction. Teri is a very empathic person. Discernment is one of her gifts. She can quickly see into the heart and feel the pain of others. Teri is comfortable in one-on-one and small-group situations.

I, on the other hand, love a party. The more, the merrier. Bounding through the kitchen door after work, I often ask: "What are we doing tonight? Who can we go out with?" Teri reminds me it is a school night for our kids, and they need our help with homework. I am not only comfortable in larger groups, but I also thrive on them.

Teri and I have learned that our personalities are a driving force behind our social dimension. We understand that Teri's energy is drained during group activity, but I gain energy through group interaction. Respecting each other's natural bent socially has been a process resulting in a greater degree of balance for each of us.

The social dimension of life can be overemphasized, and it can be underemphasized. Overemphasizing our social dimension can cause us to be overbearing. Underemphasizing our social dimension can leave the impression that we are not interested in relationships. The key to living a balanced life in your social dimension is understanding your personality and growing it to develop meaningful relationships.

3. BUILD CAPACITY

We are told that saving money is important because we never really know when an emergency might necessitate its use. When we save, we build capacity that is free to respond when needed.

Our four dimensions work in the same way. When we deplete our physical dimension, we crash. When we emphasize our intellectual dimension to the exclusion of our social dimension, we find there is no one with whom to share the fruits of our labor. When we fail to make deposits in our spiritual life, we find nothing to draw on when flattened by a crisis.

Balance is achieved when we establish, build, and maintain capacity in each of the four dimensions of life. Capacity can be established by imposing time zones on each dimension. A time zone declaring the number of hours you will work each day ensures you have time to devote to your other three dimensions and helps build capacity for those seasons in your work life when more hours are truly necessary to get the job done. Setting up a time zone around your physical activity guarantees your follow-through and at the same time helps you avoid burnout, which is usually fatal to an exercise program. Determining a spiritual time zone is critical because this dimension is easily and often forgotten, even by the most spiritual. Wrapping a time zone around your social dimension is important for the overbearing if they (we) want to keep our friends. For those who are happier with themselves and by themselves, a social time zone reminds them that fellowship is essential.

The Importance of Purpose in Practice

Money in the bank gives us the capacity to spend when necessary and invest when profitable. Establishing time zones for our four dimensions ensures the capacity we need to understand, grow toward, and accomplish our purpose.

The character equation is a process of developing our practice of life in order to understand and live out our purpose in life. If we practice a meaningful life, we grow in our understanding of our purpose. Understanding our purpose and how to practice it is revealed to us one step at a time. If we deplete our capacity in any one area, we may miss an opportunity to understand our purpose better. For instance, depleting our social dimension may cause the loss of friends who through their wisdom and experience could have helped achieve our purpose. Depleting our physical dimension could result in our life being cut short.

Practicing balance gives us the capacity to accomplish and live out our purpose. How is your balance?

Apply the Character Equation

1. How is your purpose lived out in each of the four dimensions? Next, how should your purpose be lived out in each of the four dimensions? Wrap a time zone around each dimension, being sure to build in capacity for balance.
   Intellectual
   Physical
   Spiritual
   Social

2. Reflect on the following continuums and place an *X* where you are today and a check mark where you would like to be.

Play _____ Work

Intellectual

Couch Potato _____ Jim Nasium

Physical

Dead _____ Alive

Spiritual

Poor _____ Good

Relationships

EIGHT

A = Accountability

MY DAY AT THE OFFICE

t approximately 2:45 P.M. on that fateful day at the office, I was notified that an employee, Clarence, tested positive for cocaine use. That was hard news to receive. Not only was I already feeling trampled like the guy at the bottom of the pile of about one hundred people fighting for Mark McGwire's seventieth home-run ball, but the devastating human toll of drug abuse was also becoming all too familiar. I had seen others fight the problem, and I knew what Clarence had ahead of him.

Clarence had walked this road before. He knew drugs, especially cocaine, were a problem. He knew better than to hang out with his old friends. He knew that being close to his weakness increased the probability that he would give in again. He also knew the pain cocaine had caused him and that the pain of using again would only compound the problems of his prior use. He knew, but he failed to take responsibility to grow beyond his problem. Clarence played once again with cocaine, and he got burned.

Clarence had a weakness for drugs; and when that weakness joined forces with Purpose Deficiency Syndrome, the result was disastrous. When Clarence declared the Purpose Deficiency Syndrome motto, "whatever!" he followed life wherever it led. His strongest urges navigated the course; and when Clarence woke up, he was at a place in life he hated. Once again Clarence was using drugs.

THE NEED FOR ACCOUNTABILITY

WHO IS TO BLAME?

That is what happens when we succumb to Purpose Deficiency Syndrome. We wake up one day and ask, "How did I get in this situation?"

59

We come to our senses, shake our heads in disgust, and wonder aloud, "How did this happen?" We quite naturally look around for someone to blame. We point our finger at others, but as the saying goes, "Every time you point one finger at someone else, three fingers are pointing back at you!"

THE MEDIA?

Had Clarence experienced his problem a few decades ago, his chances of dodging the drug abuse bullet may have been higher. Those were the days of *The Andy Griffith Show* when millions of Americans cuddled with their families around the television to watch the antics of Barney, Andy, and Opie. *The Andy Griffith Show* entertained us and at the same time taught us how to practice life. One show might stress the need for forgiveness. Another show might emphasize the need for honesty. Others clearly taught the value of relationships.

My Three Sons, Leave It to Beaver, Gunsmoke, and *Bonanza* joined the television lineup of entertaining programs purposed to shape our culture in positive ways. By mentioning these icons of the past, you might feel I am stuck there. Not at all. There is good programming today, but more programming today displays little regard for the ideals that make for a healthy practice of life. Today, if a family watches a program together, the parents are likely to be put in a position to qualify the statement of a character or to turn down the volume in certain places so the kids will be spared the language. All too often we encounter kidlike characters humorously showing disrespect for adults. We see characters dispose of one relationship without remorse and go on to the next.

The proliferation of the twenty-four-hour news program has proved the adage, "Fact is more interesting than fiction." CNN is the most watched network in our home. Teri and I are news junkies. While much of that network's programming is suitable, even advantageous, for our kids, much of its content is not even suitable for Teri and me. The details of President Clinton's affair with Monica Lewinsky are an example.

The world seems to be a different place today from the world I knew while watching those old favorites with my family. I do not remember drug abuse, especially among kids, to be as rampant at that time. I do not remember violence in schools and in society in general to be as widespread in those earlier days as it is today. I cannot imagine interrupting *Bonanza* with the graphic descriptions of the Clinton-Lewinsky affair.

The reason our world today is a different, poorer place with respect to life's practice is not exclusively the fault of the media pressing the edge of the censorship envelope. Today's portrayal of prolific sex, drug abuse without consequence, broken relationships as a norm, and unashamed reporting of salacious facts is, in part, the design of programmers and, in part, an accurate retelling of the condition of our country.

YOU AND ME?

Ultimately the poor practice of life told through the stories of the fictitious characters of Hollywood, and the facts reported of a real but fallen person are your responsibility and my responsibility. Ultimately we are the problem and must take our share of the blame for the condition of our culture and for the failure of the Clarences we know.

Most of us see the weaknesses of others and never consider the possibility that we too could harbor similar faults. When we see a weakness or problem and move on without engaging the potential of its impact on us, that weakness or problem seems a little less important or relevant. Watching a prime-time program that includes a more intimate scene than had appeared before could elicit your rage. "I cannot believe they showed that!" you might exclaim. If you do not act to prevent a similar showing in the future, you may become resigned to such programming. Writing a letter to the CEO of the network protesting the program is such an action. Another appropriate action is simply not watching the program in the future. Either way you have acted to prevent the showing of the program in your home. If you fail to take such an action, you may wake up one day and wonder why so much of your life resembles the program you were, at one time, so upset about. Failing to act on weaknesses and problems dulls our sensitivity to them, leading to a point where we ultimately accept them.

Massachusetts Mutual Life Insurance Company commissioned a survey of American family values. The results were revealing. Well over 80 percent of the respondents believed values such as providing emotional support for your family, taking responsibility for your actions, and showing respect for your parents, children, and others were strong in their family; but only about 30 percent of these respondents felt these values were strong in their community.[1] We see the problems and weaknesses in others but fail to see many of the same weaknesses in ourselves.

The Massachusetts Mutual study supports my belief that we are good at pointing the finger at others while forgetting three fingers are pointing back at us. We are experts at watching the evening news report about the escalating problem of drug abuse in our society, acknowledging the problem by expressing thanks that drugs are not an issue in our home, then flipping the channel to something more entertaining (possibly a rerun of *The Andy Griffith Show*).

We encounter the facts of a weakness, then move on without asking the hard questions about how that weakness might apply to our lives. Then one day we wake up, and we come to our senses when one of our kids is Clarence. Maybe it is one of our friends. Perhaps we have become Clarence. It is then we ask, "How did this happen?" When confronted with the facts initially, we should have asked, "What can I do to keep this from happening to me or someone I know?" We should act before the downward spiral of Purpose Deficiency Syndrome takes hold.

INTERVENING THROUGH ACCOUNTABILITY

A pencil is useless until it is sharpened because the blunt end of a pencil cannot make a mark. The pencil becomes useful when it is subjected to the sharpening blades of a pencil sharpener. Sharpening is a process of shaving away the useless layers of wood around the lead until the useful point is established.

Sheep live according to the same principle. The wool that protects the sheep during the winter must be removed before summer. Otherwise the wool would prevent the sheep's body heat from dissipating, and the sheep would die. Sheep kick and bleat when sheared for the first time. As the sheep lives during the months following the shearing, they learn the value of the shearing process. Beginning with the second shearing, the sheep stand quietly, allowing the shearer to complete the task.[2] Why? Because the sheep learn the life-giving nature of being sheared.

We need to be sheared of those weaknesses that can cause us to fall. We need to cut away all the layers of our lives that conflict with our purpose. We need to be sharpened so our practice of life will match our purpose in life. We cannot shear ourselves; we need help with the process. Solomon wrote, "As iron sharpens iron, so one man sharpens another" (Prov. 27:17). That is the point of accountability—caring enough about another person to respectfully shear away the weak layers of life.

Clarence knew he had a weakness, but he never openly allowed another person to help him shear it away. He failed to become accountable. Many people wake up and ask, "How did this happen?" Through the help of a trusted friend calling them into account, these same people could have averted the disaster.

BECOMING ACCOUNTABLE

Like much of life, accountability is a choice. No one can force you to become accountable because accountability by its nature is a process of entrusting yourself, your weaknesses, your strengths, your thoughts, your desires, your hopes, your fears, and your actions to the counsel and wisdom of another person. Three steps are necessary to become accountable:

1. Accept responsibility to live a purposeful life.
2. Raise the bar of the acceptable practice of life.
3. Reach out to a trusted partner.

1. ACCEPT RESPONSIBILITY TO LIVE A PURPOSEFUL LIFE

Clarence has a weakness saying no to drugs. But Clarence can say no to drugs if he chooses to. A trusted ally to hold him accountable is needed. But first Clarence must decide that he is the only person who determines his actions and that his practice of life should match his purpose in life. Before we can move beyond our own weaknesses toward our purpose, we must be willing to point the finger at ourselves before pointing a finger at others.

2. RAISE THE BAR OF THE ACCEPTABLE PRACTICE OF LIFE

The numbing of our senses that results from the constant intake of images and information from media and events can cause us to lower our expectations of ourselves and those around us. One of the articles of impeachment leveled against President Nixon was that he lied to the American people. President Nixon's lie was not under oath or in some formal proceeding. President Nixon told a lie on national television while addressing the nation. Some twenty-five years later President Clinton testified in a deposition that he did not have a sexual relationship with Monica Lewinsky. Later the president addressed the nation on national television and emphatically denied any sexual relationship with Monica Lewinsky. Seven months later President Clinton admitted to the nation that he had an "inappropriate" relationship with her.

Like President Nixon, President Clinton looked Americans in the eye and told a lie. Nixon would have been impeached had he not resigned. Clinton, on the other hand, is defended by lawyers and others who say: "Sure he lied; but, come on, does it really matter? Does his lie have anything to do with his running the country?"

In twenty-five short years America has begun to measure morality with a sliding scale. We have watched one scandal after another and failed to act. We have seen one weakness after another, and we reasoned that others might be affected, but *we* are not affected so why worry. In the midst of the Clinton scandal, many have asked, "How did this happen? How did we get here?" Now that we are "here," where are we? Location maps in amusement parks use the phrase, "You are here." What if we had such an indicator for morality's sliding scale?

"Here" is a place where tolerance is the disguise for indifference. "Here" the question is, Does a lie really matter? It is "here" that the Purpose Deficiency Syndrome motto, "whatever!" is heard. "Here" is where we give in and give up the good habits and keep the bad habits.

"Here" we place other's affirmation of us above our purpose. We long to be affirmed by others so we go along to get along. We accept less than our own and another person's best because we fear the tension that could result from attempting to hold that person accountable.

Ballard Middle School in Macon, Georgia, spent some time "here." During the 1994–1995 school year, 80 percent of the seventh grade averaged Ds or Fs. "Here" says that if you want to make Ds and Fs, go ahead. The school's leaders grew tired of "here"; and when "here" did not work any longer, their leaders sought change. The school gave the kids a choice in the fall of 1995. "If they passed six challenging courses, performed community service and had a flawless behavior record, they would complete two years of school work in one year and move on directly to the ninth grade. Two-thirds of the program's participants—last year's trouble-makers—are on the honor roll. Teacher Tracy Dye says the higher expectations changed them."[3]

Raising expectations can light a fire in the life of a Purpose Deficiency Syndrome victim. Raising the bar can give hope to those who cannot see purpose and start them on the journey to a better life.

3. REACH OUT TO A TRUSTED PARTNER

You cannot shear yourself, and you cannot grow to the heights possible through the character equation without accountability. You are left with one option: Entrust yourself to a friend. Step 3 of becoming accountable requires vulnerability.

Becoming vulnerable can be frightening. Laying yourself open to another person is not a natural act, and you should not take this process lightly. Choosing the right person is critical. Look for three characteristics:

1. Look for someone who truly cares about you.
2. Look for someone who is willing to be accountable to you just as you are accountable to him or her.
3. Look for someone you can trust.

Once you have identified a trusted friend, set a time and place to meet. Schedule a regular meeting and follow through on the scheduled times. Building the kind of intimacy that produces true vulnerability takes time. Trust is the key, and experience is the platform on which it is produced. Without trust, vulnerability is not only impossible, but it is also unwarranted. Never, ever violate the confidence of your partner.

THE IMPORTANCE OF PRACTICE IN PURPOSE

Clarence did not understand the issue of accountability. He did not see the life-giving benefit of entrusting himself to another person. Thus, Clarence failed to accept responsibility for his actions. He was too busy playing the role of the victim. Why, then, consider raising the bar? Standards, much less higher standards, have no relevance to the Purpose Deficiency Syndrome-prone. When Clarence reached out, it was not to entrust himself to another person. Rather, Clarence reached out for help buying more cocaine. The cycle, the downward spiral, continued.

Clarence's tale is common. Purpose Deficiency Syndrome leaves people feeling that there is no way out and no one to help them. Of course, that is a lie. Relationships based on mutual accountability help people stay on course toward their purpose. Some people need help just to get on the road. All of us need help to maintain our course once on the road to purpose. We judge ourselves by our intentions; others judge us by our actions. The practice of accountability seeks to ensure our practice complies with our purpose.

APPLY THE CHARACTER EQUATION

1. What role does accountability play in your life?
2. List a few areas where you may be weak. (For example, pornography, financial matters, communication, quality of work, etc.)
3. List the people in your life whom you consider "trusted friends."
4. With which one of these people are you most comfortable sharing intimate issues?
5. Invite the person listed in question 4 to join you in a mutually accountable relationship.

NINE

$$S_{1} = Service$$

MY DAY AT THE OFFICE

*D*anny gave every indication he was running a marathon, that he was prepared to go the distance in his career. That day at the office, just before lunch, I learned that Danny was a sprinter. Danny carelessly left company checks out on his credenza in open view of anyone wandering through the office he managed. The checks must have lit up like a neon sign to the person looking for a free lunch. Someone picked up the checks and began cashing them all over town. Danny had no idea the checks were missing.

Like several of the incidents during that day at the office, this was not the first indication Danny was struggling to survive. Telephone calls to Danny were not returned promptly. Customer satisfaction with Danny's office had begun to drop. The incident with the checks confirmed what I suspected. Danny had developed a classic case of Purpose Deficiency Syndrome. He was doing only enough to get by. Danny had grown tired of his responsibilities and had become indifferent to the needs of his customers. Although his service at one time was excellent, it was now ineffective.

THE NEED FOR SERVICE

Studies indicate that about 70 percent of customers who quit doing business with a company do so because of an attitude of indifference toward them by one employee of the firm.[1] The attitude of indifference is nearly impossible to conceal. Entering a restaurant, you are greeted and seated by a bubbly hostess who turns the table over to a stone-faced waiter. "Maybe he is having a bad day," you reason, but when he forgets the third request for ketchup, you know this is a problem—a Purpose Deficiency Syndrome-induced indifference.

Facial expression is not the only clue to the possibility of indifferent, ineffective service. Tone of voice is a clear indicator of attitude. You can visualize the smoke bellowing from the mouth and nostrils of the attendant as she huffs and puffs under her breath at your request to be transferred to another person. Closing the blinds at 4:50 P.M. when the store is supposed to close at 5:00 P.M. is an action of indifference toward the purpose and practice of a person's work.

Purpose Deficiency Syndrome is a serious problem to the life of organizations because its victims (the organization's employees) almost always exhibit indifference. Studies show that indifference is the leading cause of lost customers. That is one reason the practice of service is so important in the character equation. People of character recognize that customers are people who have a need. The character equation calls the person of character to move beyond his indifference to see the many needs of the people he encounters and to muster the energy to meet the needs.

IMPROVING YOUR SERVICE

The character equation defines a process of growing our strength to live a purposeful life. Some days indifference sets in, and we wonder if it is possible to overcome it. Here is a five-step process to dumping indifference and improving your service:

1. Change your perspective.
2. Understand the needs of your customer.
3. Get involved.
4. Celebrate when needs are met.
5. Develop an expectation statement.

1. CHANGE YOUR PERSPECTIVE

Our perspectives about ourselves, our coworkers, customers, performance, education, change, and tasks shape the depth and scope of service we provide. Service begins before we enter the work domain. Service begins the moment we wake. From that moment forward our perspective is in constant formation and can be generally locked in with the first encounter of the day. A proper perspective is essential to the practice of service.

Employee to Contributor

Danny was in that often perplexing position of management where he was both employee and employer. As an employee, Danny viewed his role solely in the context of the subordinate. Purpose Deficiency Syndrome prevented him from seeing the enormous contribution he had made in his role. But for Danny, the word *employee* carried little pizzazz, little energy. Over time, Danny the employee lost interest and woke up wondering how he allowed the checks to be stolen.

Danny's story is interesting and typical because the very attitude that led him to repeated error also is an indication of his capacity and desire for a life of character. Danny wanted more responsibility, which is a mark of a person in search of a purposeful life. But that desire for more responsibility was infected by the Purpose Deficiency Syndrome perspective that being "an employee" limited his contribution. Purpose Deficiency Syndrome prevented Danny from seeing the wonderful opportunities to serve in his current position.

Danny needed to change his perspective from employee to contributor. A contributor is important to the team. Contributors notice that others listen when they speak because contributors have something valuable to share. Contributors speak with confidence which helps others listen. Contributors serve their customers with zeal because they know they are meeting an important need.

Employer to Steward

Danny managed ten people in a branch office. He was given a lot of autonomy to manage his office. His position, together with the free hand to manage, created an unlimited opportunity to serve those in his charge. Instead Danny looked on his people as a burden to carry. When an employee had a medical need, Danny saw the forms that had to be completed and the disruption of his office. He could have seen the opportunity to meet the need of the employee. When an employee made a mistake, he saw the error instead of seeing the opportunity to use the error as a way to improve his office.

A steward is a person who manages on behalf of another. Stewards have overcome Purpose Deficiency Syndrome and are strengthening the character in the purpose and practice of life. Stewards infect their cultures with an energetic desire to serve. Stewards know their calling is to serve those in their charge.

Activity to Results

Danny's perspective about performance led him to conclude the point of his work was his activity instead of his results. This perspective is both the product of Purpose Deficiency Syndrome and a cause of Purpose Deficiency

Syndrome. It is from this perspective that a person reasons that doing just enough to get by is all that is required. Working from this perspective, Danny blindly followed the checklist for given procedures. He rarely asked questions that could uncover a systemic problem. Danny just went about his eight-to-five routine believing that his performance would be judged as adequate if he completed the required activity.

There are two problems with this perspective. First, in any relationship, work, or home, an implied expectation exists that the participants will do more than what is required to maintain the status quo. Completing your assigned activity on your own, then, cannot be judged as adequate performance. Second, mistakes are inevitable. If you have added value to the activity, you are preparing in advance for future mistakes and will have stored up trust and confidence in your abilities. That was Danny's problem when the checks were stolen. Danny had added little value to the activity of his office. There was no "extra credit" to draw on when his management was called into question.

People of character are not satisfied with the mere activity of their work. They desire results from their service to customers. In fact, people of character desire to serve; they pant for opportunities; they thrive on opportunities; and when such an opportunity is not apparent, they seek to create an opportunity.

People of character seeking to serve their customers may find the results desired by their employer to be somewhat different from the results called for in the character equation. Businesses often define results in easily quantifiable terms. The character equation certainly seeks to quantify the result but often extends the definition beyond the requirements of an employer. For example, a person in sales might be told his desired result or performance is measured by the sale of so many units of a product. The character equation extends that definition by adding to the number of units an understanding of how the product met the need of the customer. Thus, people seeking to solve the character equation should always be highly motivated and energized by their results because their service opportunities and their results are directly correlated.

If our perspective about our customers is negative, our service to them will most likely be poor (if we serve them at all). If our perspective is that our task is limited to a narrow list, we might miss the opportunity to serve in other areas of interest.

Training to Learning

I am often engaged in training classes for clients of my consulting practice. In the first fifteen minutes I can separate the class between those who came to be trained and those who came to learn. There is a difference, and almost without exception the people coming to be trained are struggling with Purpose Deficiency Syndrome while the learners have kicked the Purpose Deficiency Syndrome habit with the help of the character equation.

If a course were scheduled by his employer, Danny would attend but only after being told it was required. He would arrive about one minute after the announced starting time as a public declaration of his desire to be anywhere else at the time. Sitting in the back of the room, his eyes would signal that his brain was wandering back to last weekend's game. At the end of the day, Danny's workbook pages would be as clean as when he entered the room. His indifference would act as a dare as if to say, "Go ahead and train me!"

Learners come into the class smiling. They are anticipating something new, excited by the possibility of walking away with even a single fresh idea. Learners understand that results are the point of activity and that learning is the point of training. To learn, the learner knows his investment in the class through participation, questions, brainstorming, and discussion is necessary. Learners know that learning is necessary if service is the objective. Providing service to a person in need often requires the server to stretch in areas yet to be mastered. The perspective of learning is critical to service.

Crisis to Opportunity

Purpose Deficiency Syndrome causes people to view any change as a crisis. We decided to expand Danny's office a few years before the incident with the checks. To our amazement Danny resisted the change even though the change in the amount of space for his department was increasing. Though it was in his favor, it was still change; and Danny's perspective was that change is not good. So he behaved like so many Purpose Deficiency Syndrome sufferers behave in the midst of change. He erected barriers; he stalled; and he came up with alternatives.

The service-minded would have viewed the increased space as an opportunity to serve their employees and their customers. They would have imagined several new ways to position the offices so the space would be more accessible to customers. People of character see change as an opportunity to serve others while enhancing the practice of their purpose.

Customer with Money to Customer with Need

Danny came to view his customers as mere commodities. They were, to Danny, people with money who bought our product. He acted toward them as if they, the customers, were there to serve him. Danny misunderstood the point of the relationship with the customers. The customers have a need, and that is why we have the opportunity to serve them. If we enthusiastically meet their needs, perhaps we will have the opportunity to serve them again. If we approach their needs with indifference, there is a 70 percent probability we will lose them as customers. If we lose them as customers, we lose the opportunity to meet their needs. Meeting needs is the objective of service, and this practice of service is a powerful factor in the character equation.

2. UNDERSTAND THE NEEDS OF YOUR CUSTOMER

Usually we begin a consulting relationship by profiling our client's corporate culture. One of the areas of the profile addresses this practice of service and specifically the depth of understanding of the needs of the customer. We find that many firms think they understand the needs of their customers but in reality have only a shallow view of these needs.

Taken on face value, a customer's needs may appear obvious and simple. Take the customer of a stock brokerage, as an example. Her needs would appear to be finding places to park a sum of money. Certainly that is her request of the stockbroker, but her need is much deeper. She has a need to invest for retirement in a few years. That information is good for the stockbroker to know, but her need runs even deeper. Her need is to find stability and consistency in life. For this customer, as with most people, investing money is stressful. The stockbroker can meet her need by understanding the ultimate use of the money, investing it with an appropriate tolerance for risk, then spending the time to explain fully the investment strategy. The opportunity to meet her needs continues; the stockbroker can stay in touch with his client, keeping her abreast of developments. That is service. Had the stockbroker simply asked a few superficial questions, he may never have truly understood his customer's need.

Fully understanding the customer's needs is tough. Often you literally have to pull the needs out of the customer. Suppose your customer is "internal." That is, your customer works for your same employer in the next department. Your work product, a mortgage file, is passed on to that department. Asking your internal customer to describe his need might elicit a response such as, "I need the documents in the file in this order when the file arrives." But is that the real need?

Probing deeper, you learn your internal customer is a single parent who must pick up her child at a certain time each day. You learn that, her department has a standing rule that a certain number of files have to be worked each day before employees clock out. You learn that, if the files you send her are not in good order, it slows her down to the point she cannot work her required number of files before 5 P.M. You learn that poor service on your part results in her being late to pick up her son. Your service opportunity is to help your internal customer pick up her son who eagerly awaits her arrival every day! You cannot fully serve your customer until you fully understand the need.

3. GET INVOLVED

Danny was known to be the quiet type in a meeting. He sat through most meetings never uttering a word. For a long time most of us thought he was shy. We learned however that his few words had more to do with his Purpose Deficiency Syndrome-induced indifference. He was unattached to the process; therefore, he waited for someone to make a decision and give him a directive.

Getting involved in the decisions of your company comes naturally when you change your perspective, really understand the needs of your customer, and step out boldly to serve them. Through service you experience your purpose.

- Get involved by being prepared, ready for company discussions. Give others the benefit of your experience. Learn from the experience of others.
- Get involved by unleashing your creativity. Adults tend to suppress their creativity. You are uniquely gifted, and your customers and coworkers would benefit from your using your creativity.
- Get involved by testing your ideas on small groups before rolling them out to large groups. Verify your instincts. Find the best way to meet a need.
- Get involved by making the changes necessary to meet the most needs. Do not take on the pride of authorship. Realize that your work, your creativity, is a gift.
- Get involved by rolling out your product to as many people as possible who need it.

4. CELEBRATE MET NEEDS

Celebrating when the needs of a person are met is impossible for the Purpose Deficiency Syndrome victim. Purpose Deficiency Syndrome blinds you to the need as well as the recognition that a need has been met. Reinforcing the positive power of meeting needs is one way to hold Purpose Deficiency Syndrome at bay. The celebration should be simple, such as bringing lunch in for the department. Perhaps sharing the news with a friend would be a good way to mark the occasion. The point is to punctuate the moment with positive reinforcement.

5. DEVELOP AN EXPECTATION STATEMENT

Meeting needs is not always easy. Some days we do not feel like serving others. For those days it is good to have issued an expectation statement.

An expectation statement is a written declaration of the type and quality of service your customer should expect. This statement sets the expectations of your customer and provides you with some level of accountability to ensure that expectations are met, if not exceeded. The expectation statement raises the bar of acceptable service. Further, this statement is a good way to discern if your product or service is suitable for your customer.

THE IMPORTANCE OF PRACTICE IN PURPOSE

Service lights the fires of passion as we meet the needs of our customers. Through service we experience our purpose. Through serving others we discover and develop our inborn abilities. By serving others we develop our relationships.

The practice of service keeps our perspective fixed on our purpose. The practice of service calls us to engage in the activity of our work in ways that strengthen our character. In the end, serving others teaches us how to live a purposeful life, then gives us the energy to do it. Eric Liddell, the runner whose life was portrayed in the movie *Chariots of Fire*, was quoted as saying, "God made me fast; and when I run, I feel his pleasure." We are made for service; and when we serve, we feel "his pleasure."

APPLY THE CHARACTER EQUATION

1. Mark where you are on each continuum.

   Employee _ Contributor
   Employer _ Steward
   Activity _ Results
   Training _ Learning
   Crisis   _ Opportunity
   Customer with $$$ _ _ _ _ _ _ _ _ _ _ _ _ _ _ _ _ Customer with need

   If you are to the left of center on any of these continuums, make today the turning point in your perspective.

2. List your "customers" at work and at home.
3. What are the true needs of your customers? What changes are required for you to meet these needs?
4. Write your expectation statement.

74

TEN

C = Communication

MY DAY AT THE OFFICE

I thought I was safe. I had escaped my office and the hiss of my phone. I rounded the corner, and my car was in sight. But blocking my path stood two managers, Jane and Tom, nose to nose in a heated argument. Maybe it was the striped shirt I was wearing that compelled them to draw me in to mediate the conflict.

The conflict between these two good managers was typical of most conflicts I refereed. Tom had made comments over time that annoyed Jane, but she stuffed her feelings without revealing her hurt. This scenario happened over and over. Each time Jane failed to speak up, her feelings inflated her emotional balloon. After a number of encounters, Jane's emotional balloon filled, a misunderstanding between their departments played the part of the pin, and the once-quiet Jane popped off on a verbal tirade like a once-filled balloon screaming through the air.

THE NEED TO COMMUNICATE

Tom's and Jane's impasse was not the result of some procedural problem. It was these two managers' inabilities to communicate that led to the breakdown. Their conflict was typical of the type of conflict I often mediated in that mortgage company, and it is typical of the conflict we work to resolve today in our client organizations. The issue is almost always communication.

Communication never just happens; it is an intentional act. Purpose Deficiency Syndrome keeps us from acknowledging our responsibility to be good communicators. Purpose Deficiency Syndrome leads its victims to act only in their own self-interest; and with 80 percent of the workforce infected with the disease, it is understandable why today's workplace culture is often marked by incivility and often high turnover levels.

"Companies are no longer like small towns or neighborhoods where people work with others for years, and trust and understanding of people's foibles and personalities develop. Today, companies are more like cities, where people come in and leave."[1] There seems to be less time today to develop intimate friendships at work which, among other things, improve communication. Adding to the problem is the impersonal nature of our communication style today brought on by the development of the tools such as E-mail, voice mail, and the Internet.

Ironically these efficient tools for delivering messages has, for many people, become the excuse for communication breakdowns. I hear and deliver this message and others like it too often: "You left a message in my voice mail? Funny, I never received it." Phone tag is the most frequently played corporate game today. E-mail, voice mail, and the other tools help us deliver messages more efficiently, but they do not cure poor communication. Nonverbal communication such as eye contact and posture account for approximately 90 percent of communication. Therefore, the great advances in technology are only improving about 10 percent of communication. These tools are great, but they do not communicate. People communicate.

Communication is confirmed understanding. People communicate when we make an intentional effort to know, understand, and give of ourselves to others. Communication is the key to turning our workplace cultures from an attitude of, "We are all in this alone," to an attitude of, "We are all in this together."

THE CHARACTER OF EFFECTIVE COMMUNICATION

I have little to add to the volumes of good material that have been written on the techniques of effective communication. Our purpose is basic. Here we are wrestling with three principles that must be present for the techniques of communication to be effective. The three principles are:

1. Think of others as greater than yourself.
2. Understand how you and others naturally communicate.
3. Shift your natural communication style to the natural style of others.

1. THINK OF OTHERS AS GREATER THAN YOURSELF

The demands and stress of our work often cause us to focus only on our task and our needs. We place our needs above the needs of others. We are stressed into selfishness, which is the beginning of breakdown in communication.

Tom and Jane could have benefited from this wisdom from Dale Carnegie, "You can make more friends in two months by becoming interested in other people than you can in two years by trying to get other people interested in you." Thinking and acting on the needs of others instead of your own is unselfishness.

Unselfishness demonstrates respect for others and clears the air for true communication. Instead of needling each other for one more favor, one more "what can you do for me?" request, Jane and Tom should have focused on "what can I do for you?" Such an attitude would have created positive shared experiences based on respect for each other. That understanding of mutual respect facilitates the clean resolution of conflict. People who have built mutual respect bring to the conflict table a confirmed understanding of the worth and intent of the other party. Gone are the concerns about motive and "what is he not saying?" Such concerns plagued Tom and Jane, making communication or a confirmed understanding of the other's position impossible. Without communication, resolution was not and is not possible. Communication begins when we build mutual respect by considering others greater than ourselves.

2. Understand How You and Others Naturally Communicate

Communication is built on mutual respect and improved as we learn our natural communication styles. For example, I understand best if a person literally draws me a picture. Others understand best by hearing and still others by reading. I am prone to give others quick instructions for a task, but I take hours explaining the happenings of an event. Others are much more detailed when explaining a task but quick to the point when discussing an event. Knowing my natural communication style helps me communicate in a way that leads to confirmed understanding.

One way to understand your natural communication style is by understanding your personality type. The way we communicate is largely dependent on our personality. Is an introverted person usually a verbose communicator? Does the hard-charging, type A person usually take a lot of time explaining directions for a task? There is a correlation between personality type and communication style.

Studies of the human personality date back to the fifth century B.C. Hippocrates believed that four natural forces—earth, water, air, and fire— controlled human behavior and that these four forces corresponded to four dimensions of human personality. Galen, another Greek physician, gave life to the four dimensions of human personality by naming them sanguine, choleric, melancholic, and phlegmatic. Since the time of Hippocrates and Galen, these four dimensions of human personality have been tested and proven.[2]

Today a number of systems exist, based on the four-dimensional model, that profile a person's personality. John Trent and Gary Smalley presented one of the most interesting systems. Trent and Smalley delightfully bring the subject of personality to life, and I am using their model in this discussion of personality and communication styles.[3]

Discover Your Personality Style

Learning the basics of personality style will help you understand how you naturally communicate. You need to understand these basics if you seek to communicate clearly and effectively with others. The information presented here is designed to illustrate the point of the link between personality and communication. The point here is this: while your communication style depends on your personality, you can control your communication to make it effective in others' lives. A number of personality profile systems are more in-depth, applying personality not only to communication style but also to stress, interpersonal relationships, ability to work on a team, etc.[4]

In the following survey, circle the words in each block that are most like you. Circle as many as apply. Next, add up the number of words and phrases you circled in each box. Now double your score to come up with a total for each box. Finally, take the scores from each box and transfer them to the graph below the survey. Lastly, connect the dots on the graph.

As you take this short self-survey, keep two things in mind. First, circle the words that most consistently describe you. Second, be sure to circle the words that describe the way you are and not the way you want to be. You could make yourself look like the person you always wanted to be but that would not help you move in that direction. To become the person you always wanted to be, you must first acknowledge who you are today. Have fun!

Plot your scores on the graph and connect the dots. What does this all mean? The four letters at the top of each section stand for one of the four personality dimensions. Each holds a key to understanding how we communicate. The graph indicates that each person is a combination of the four dimensions.

Personal Strengths Survey Chart

ℒ

Takes Charge	Bold
Determined	Purposeful
Assertive	Decision Maker
Firm	Leader
Enterprising	Goal-driven
Competitive	Self-reliant
Enjoys Challenges	Adventurous

"Let's do it now!"

Double the number circled ____

ℬ

Deliberate	Discerning
Controlled	Detailed
Reserved	Analytical
Predictable	Inquisitive
Practical	Precise
Orderly	Persistent
Factual	Scheduled

"How was it done in the past?"

Double the number circled ____

𝒪

Takes risks	Fun-loving
Visionary	Likes Variety
Motivator	Enjoys Change
Energetic	Creative
Very Verbal	Group-oriented
Promoter	Mixes Easily
Avoids Details	Optimistic

"Trust me! It'll work out!"

Double the number circled ____

𝒢

Loyal	Adaptable
Nondemanding	Sympathetic
Even Keel	Thoughtful
Avoids Conflict	Nurturing
Enjoys Routine	Patient
Dislikes Change	Tolerant
Deep Relationships	Good Listener

"Let's keep things the way they are"

Double the number circled ____

	ℒ	ℬ	𝒪	𝒢
30				
15				
0				

L = Lion

If your highest score is in the "L" category, you probably identify with the doers known as Lions. If you are interested in results, you are looking for a lion; but be careful because they can be insensitive to the needs and accomplishments of others. Lions thrive on competition and usually make their way to the top of the corporate food chain. Lions are impatient and intolerant of people who waste time.

Lions naturally communicate by:
- Giving facts in the form of bullet points (guess which dimension dominates my personality)
- Providing short, concise, bottom-line, unemotional answers to questions
- Confronting a problem directly.

Lions respond poorly to communication that:
- Is wordy
- Interrupts their activity
- Beats around the bush
- Rambles on and on

B = Beaver

A high score in the "B" category identifies you as a beaver. Beavers are the conscientious members of the group. They have studied all the rules and instructions and believe it is their duty not only to see that the job is done but that the job is done right. Beavers are detail oriented in their quest for the facts and rarely let a time deadline take priority over accuracy. Beavers tend to be perfectionists.

Beavers naturally communicate by:
- Providing detailed explanations and information
- Offering critical analysis
- Qualifying their opinions in the event (though Beavers believe it is unlikely they are wrong)

Beavers respond poorly to communication that is:
- Pushy
- Disrespectful toward them
- Too vague

O = Otter

A high score in the "O" category means you are an Otter. Otters are the life of the party. They live to influence people and thrive on group activities. Otters seem to "fly by the seat of their pants," acting on intuition and gut feel. Otters are known to overcommit themselves and often lose track of time. Otters make friends easily.

Otters naturally communicate by:
- Expressing kindness and affirmation
- Casting a vision without a lot of detail

- Prioritizing people over tasks

Otters respond poorly to communication that is:
- Unkind, insensitive, and judgmental
- Too oriented toward a task versus people
- Too detailed

G = Golden Retriever

Golden retrievers score high on the "G" category. Golden retrievers are loyal listeners. "Feeling your pain" is their strength. These people have the gift of encouragement and are willing to give it often to those in their lives. Golden retrievers are the most casual, relaxed, and adaptable of the personality types. Golden retrievers are cooperative and reliable performers who provide practical solutions. Golden retrievers can be hurt easily and have the tendency to suppress their painful feelings.

Golden retrievers naturally communicate by:
- Acknowledging others' accomplishments
- Focusing on the positive
- Addressing others' emotional pain

Golden retrievers respond poorly to communication that is:
- Demeaning and hostile
- Manipulative
- Negative

All four dimensions are present in all of us, and yet each of us is uniquely different. This unique personality blend determines our natural communication style. Knowing your personality helps you understand how you communicate and, just as importantly, how others communicate. We tend to treat others as we want to be treated, and we tend to communicate with others the way we want others to communicate with us.

Communication is confirmed understanding. That means communication occurs when all parties in the communication loop acknowledge their understanding of the message by repeating it and acting on it. The question of communication inevitably becomes the responsibility of each participant to go the extra mile to understand and to be understood. Considering others greater than yourself is the first step toward effective communication. Knowing the four personality types and how these types shape your communication is the essential next step. These two steps alone, however, do not result in communication. One more step is necessary to cross the threshold of communication consistently. Shift your natural communication style to the natural style of others.

3. ADAPT YOUR NATURAL COMMUNCIATION STYLE TO THE NATURAL STYLE OF OTHERS

This third step toward effective communication takes the perspective of step 1 and the knowledge of step 2 and puts them into action. Shifting your natural communication style to the natural style of others is not easy or natural, but that is what makes it so powerful. Why is style-shifting so powerful? Because it shows you care! Style-shifting demonstrates you highly value the other person.

Tom is a lion, and Jane is a golden retriever. Their communication breakdown could have been avoided if they had followed these three steps. Tom's natural style was to come into a meeting and take over. He pounced on people who beat around the bush. He roared at anyone who disagreed with his viewpoint. Tom's lionlike personality led him to overpower most of his coworkers through his communication. Unfortunately, Tom was not even aware that his style created stress among his nonlion associates like Jane.

Jane attended the same meetings as Tom. Whenever Tom was harsh or domineering, Jane would sink a little lower in her chair. Tom's style made her nervous. Jane was a master at working out solutions in a methodical way. She paced herself, being certain that the process of arriving at the solution did not hurt or demean anyone. In fact, Jane tried to manage the flow of her work in a way that actually built people up.

Jane respected Tom because he got results, but she always felt his style was unnecessarily harsh. Tom marveled at Jane's ability to build a team. Tom often thought Jane's team operated more like a family. Tom really liked Jane's approach but grew frustrated because he could not understand how to do it.

Tom and Jane kept their feelings about their work styles to themselves. On that day Tom had devoured one of Jane's employees, a valued team member. Jane, like all golden retrievers, could take a lot of emotional pain; but Tom crossed the line when he inflicted pain on her team member. Jane's loyalty to her employee took priority over her natural tendency to stuff her feelings and burst the floodgate of emotion. Several years of watching Tom wreak havoc gushed out in the form of direct, biting comments. Tom was astonished by Jane's direct confrontation, but it was the direct confrontation that Tom understood. Why? Because direct confrontation is Tom's natural style.

Tom and Jane would have been well served to learn style-shifting before having an emotional explosion. Style-shifting practiced consistently lets people know you care. You are communicating with others the way they like to communicate. Style-shifting also helps you develop your skill in areas where you might be weak, and it builds character in you and in your relationships.

Cynthia Tobias, in her book *The Way We Work*, observes: "If we only talk to people the way we prefer they talk back to us, and they're busy doing the same thing, chances are good that no one is truly listening. We haven't reached a common level of communication."[5] It takes character to be an effective communicator, and it builds character to be an effective communicator.

THE IMPORTANCE OF PURPOSE IN PRACTICE

You cannot achieve your purpose alone. That is one reason relationships weigh so heavily in the character equation. Communication is an important variable in the character equation because it is the practice that facilitates the achievement of your purpose. Through your communication you will help others understand your purpose; and if your communication is effective, you will enlist others to help you achieve it.

APPLY THE CHARACTER EQUATION

1. Look over the lists describing how the four dimensions naturally communicate and to what each responds poorly.
2. How should you shift your natural style to be effective with each of the other three styles?
3. Visualize a friend or family member who characterizes one of the four dimensions as you consider the most effective ways to shift your style.

ELEVEN

$\mathcal{PK}$ = Promise Keeping

MY DAY AT THE OFFICE

*L*iving a life marked by character requires acting on a person's need, not their request. My day of testing included such an opportunity. After several years of working together, I knew Darla well. She had a drinking problem. She called the office requesting a week of vacation, and her words were so slurred and run together it reminded me of a multicar fender bender on the freeway. One word seemed to bump into the one just before it, as if they were audibly hooked together.

I heard Darla's request, but I knew her vacation was a week of hanging out with Jack Daniels, Mr. Smirnoff, and an old Wild Turkey. Her request for vacation at that time meant she was drunk and wanted to stay drunk.

I heard Darla's request, but I knew Darla's need and that was my opportunity to demonstrate my character. Darla needed to be admitted to an alcohol treatment facility and begin working through the process of healing. She did not see her need. In fact, Darla was actually requesting the opportunity to immerse herself in the very thing that could kill her.

This was a moment of truth for me. Was I serious about my commitment to character? The easy decision would have been to grant Darla's request, then put her out of mind for a week. After all, I had a hundred other things to do besides addressing Darla's need. The rationalizations were forming in my mind when one simple thought brought me back to reality, *What did you promise Darla when she came to work here?* In a flash I knew what had to be done because I made (and I continue to make) a point of telling our people that I cared about them and that they could count on me to be interested in their needs.

I could have granted her request for a week of boozing it up, but my action would have breached the promise I made to Darla and others. My commitment to character necessarily meant I must keep my promise and address her need. I asked Darla, "Do you remember my telling you that I would always try to do what was in your best interest?" She did. So I continued, "Have you known me to break that promise?" She had not. So I said, "Darla, I believe you have a drinking problem and the best for you is to check into a treatment facility." Darla trusted me and checked herself into a nearby facility.

THE NEED FOR PROMISE KEEPING

The WorkCulture Profile© is a tool I use to assess the corporate culture of my clients.[1]. Among other things, the profile frequently identifies a lack of trust among employees. In essence, the cultures of these companies operate on a basis of, "I'm OK, but you are not OK." Digging deeper, we often find this lack of trust is due, at least in part, to a serious case of promise breaking. We break promises in small ways like missing a meeting or a deadline because "something came up." It was a big broken promise that changed the course of my day at work. When one person harasses another person, in this case sexually, the promise of respect for the individual is broken. Gone too are the promises of a productive, healthy work environment.

What does "something came up" and aggressive, demeaning behavior communicate to the recipient? Have you been on the receiving end of such a broken promise? If so, you know those messages clearly communicate that other things are more important to that person than you. How do you feel about a person who evades responsibility for behavior or is constantly distorting the facts?

Broken promises, big or small, can destroy trust. Trust is the foundation on which our relationships are built. Promise keeping is the adhesive, the substance of our character that prevents the foundation of trust from cracking. Purpose Deficiency Syndrome seeks to destroy trust, thereby destroying relationships. The Purpose Deficiency Syndrome victim, wandering through life without purpose, naturally becomes a promise breaker when something more appealing "comes up."

With 80 percent of the workforce suffering from Purpose Deficiency Syndrome, it is easy to understand why our relationships at work and at home are in such chaos. Employer and employee relationships should be built on the foundation of trust, but trust is clearly not evident in many workplace relationships when the number of discrimination lawsuits has increased 2,200 percent over the past two decades. What does an overall increase in employment litigation of 400 percent over the past twenty years suggest about the depth of trust today?[2] Add to it the escalating rate of divorce and an undeniable picture emerges of relationships destroyed by broken promises.

If we hope to achieve our purpose, we must have vibrant, healthy relationships. If our workplaces are going to thrive, we must have productive, growing relationships. If our homes are going to survive, we must decide to make relationships our first priority. Trust is the foundation on which all relationships are built. Promise keeping adheres the relationship to the foundation of trust. We must develop a pattern of consistent promise keeping.

MAKING PROMISE KEEPING A HABIT

Good habits, like following through on your commitments, require practice. Not only do we need to keep our promises, but we also need to keep our promises consistently, habitually, every day. Making a habit of a good behavior, such as promise keeping, requires daily focus. The following steps help break the habit of breaking promises:

1. Become a trust leader.
2. Filter your promises through your purpose statement.
3. Promise only what you can deliver.
4. Promise and deliver only what is in the best interest of the other person.

1. BECOME A TRUSTWORTHY LEADER

Darla's drinking was well-known among her friends and coworkers, but no one felt responsible to lead Darla away from the problem that plagued her. Maybe her friends felt Darla was happy in her drunken state. Perhaps they reasoned Darla's misery was of her own making, freeing them of the responsibility to get involved. Whatever their reasoning, Darla's friends proved to be untrustworthy even with the implied promise of friendship— to act in the best interest of another person. Darla needed one of her friends to step forward and accept the responsibility to become trustworthy and, by example, to lead others to become trustworthy.

Contract versus Covenant

Becoming a trustworthy leader means you accept the responsibility to keep all your promises even if others fail in keeping the promises made to you. That practice is unusual given our society's concept of contractual responsibility. It is standard procedure in the course of commerce to write a contract evidencing a business arrangement. Contracts seek to:

- Define the relationship of the parties to the contract. Their names and responsibilities are detailed.
- Define the future by spelling out the ways the contract could be broken and prescribing remedies for the default. Contracts anticipate and address problems in advance, limiting the downside risk for at least one of the parties. In that way the future is known, but it is also limited to the possibilities addressed in the contract. The future, in the context of a contract, is limited because legally binding contracts have a termination date.
- The contract is made effective through consideration or the exchange of money.

Contracts are a practical necessity and serve a useful purpose, but the underlying precept of the contract illustrates the thinking that leads to Purpose Deficiency Syndrome. Contracts are based on the notion that responsibility in a given activity or arrangement can be limited to a predefined set of actions or promises; and if those actions or promises are broken by one party, the other party is set free from responsibility.

Applying that concept to Darla's situation, we can hear her friends saying: "Darla did not show up again today. She is not holding up her end of the bargain. I am through with her." When Darla called requesting a week of vacation, we could have reasoned that she was not holding up her end of the contract and decided we would do the same. Contractually we had the right to terminate Darla; but contractual promise keeping leads to shallow, purposeless, conditional relationships.

Another paradigm yields vibrant, energetic, purposeful relationships. This paradigm is not a new theory taught by the world's promise-keeping guru. This paradigm is called covenant, and it is found in Scripture. The Bible is divided into the Old Testament and the New Testament. The word *testament* literally means "covenant." The Bible is a history of God's covenants calling people into a relationship, people continually breaking their promises to God, God always fulfilling his promises to people in spite of their failures.

Biblical covenants stand in contrast to contracts in the following ways:

- The purpose of the covenant is relationship. The covenant is the relationship unlike the contract that merely defines the relationship.
- The covenant promises an unlimited future. Unlike the contract, covenants have no termination date.
- The covenant was made effective through grace. Grace is freely giving more than is deserved. Contracts become effective with the exchange

of a stated sum of money that can be recovered if the contractual promise is broken. In spite of people's broken promises, God always kept his promises, even sacrificing his own Son as the recovered payment for our covenantal failings.

Applying this paradigm to Darla's situation yields a different result. Thinking in the context of the covenant, Darla's friends could be heard to say: "Darla did not show up again today. She is not holding up her end of the bargain, and I know she is struggling. How can we intervene and help her?"

Consider this: If the covenant is the real story, the contract is the made-for-television movie. Contracts attempt to manufacture what the covenant produces naturally. The covenant paradigm naturally yields a relationship built on the foundation of trust. I am not arguing against the use of contracts. On the contrary, use contracts but think covenant. Hold yourself to the higher standard of the covenant. Keep your promises even when others break their promises, and you will become a trust leader.

2. FILTER YOUR PROMISES THROUGH YOUR PURPOSE STATEMENT

Trust leaders know promise keeping builds trust, and trust is the basis of relationships, and relationships are central to their purpose. Trust leaders make a habit of promise keeping because it keeps them focused on their purpose.

Your purpose statement serves as a guide for making decisions and, yes, even promises. My personal purpose statement is "building faith, family, and friendship." I constantly evaluate the opportunities before me by asking the simple question, "Does this opportunity build my faith, my family, or my friendships?" Though the practical application of the process of filtering opportunities through my purpose statement is not perfect, it does provide an objective basis for making commitments in all areas of my life.

The opportunity to hire someone is a perfect use of my personal purpose statement. Certainly that decision has to be consistent with my company's needs, but it is also appropriate to test my purpose against the decision. Does adding this person build my faith, family, or friendships? is the sifting question. The answer is an emphatic yes, if I keep the promises I make by extending an employment opportunity to the prospective employee. Asking this question of personal purpose, after the corporate need has been established, helps me focus in advance on the personal commitment I am making to a prospective employee.

When Darla interviewed, we were up to our corporate eyeballs in work. We needed help—fast! If an applicant was breathing, we were ready to hire. We were overwhelmed by the growing workload and really did not want to take the time to interview a lot of people, but at times like those a deep breath and a step back yields the most reward.

The filtering process clarifies expectations. Most discussions between an employer and a prospective employee generally evolve around what the prospective employee can do for the employer. Filtering a corporate hiring decision through a personal purpose causes the employer to consider what he can do for the prospective employee. I interviewed Darla because we had a corporate need, but I filtered that hiring decision through my personal purpose, which led us to discuss my contribution to her life. Our expectations were clear. She would make a specific, measurable contribution to the company, and I committed to help her grow through our friendship at work.

The filtering process puts you in control of your circumstances. Filtering practical, everyday decisions through your purpose statement ensures you stay on track, aligned with your purpose. This process is vitally important because it prevents the common tendency to allow current circumstances to control the future.

Most people are presented with opportunities in life that on the surface appear to be good. Sometimes we are forced to make a choice between two good opportunities. You are interviewing for jobs with several companies, and two of the companies extend an offer. Both jobs look good, so which one do you choose? You are interviewing candidates for a position, and two people appear to be equally qualified. Which do you choose?

Most people live in a world where they must discern that which is good from that which is best. Oswald Chambers, in his excellent book *My Utmost for His Highest*, wrote: "Very few of us would debate over what is filthy, evil, and wrong, but we do debate over what is good. It is the good that opposes the best."[3] How do you discern good from best? Understand your purpose, and use it as a filter for making decisions and promises. The best choice will always be the choice most consistent with your purpose.

3. PROMISE ONLY WHAT YOU CAN DELIVER

This is for all the people in sales. The quickest, surest way to destroy trust is to promise today what you know you cannot deliver tomorrow. Overpromising is one of the biggest issues we see in workplaces today. Maybe people promise what they cannot deliver to get an angry customer off the phone. Perhaps the motivation is to close the sale today. Whatever the reason, overpromising establishes an expectation that will result in a broken promise and destroyed trust.

The short-term benefits of overpromising never exceed its long-term cost. You may close the sale today but lose the customer's future business. You may end the conversation with the angry customer today, but you will begin another conversation when the unhappy customer later explains your broken promise to your boss.

Purpose Deficiency Syndrome causes people to think short-term and act accordingly. Overpromising is an action based on Purpose Deficiency Syndrome, induced short-term thinking. The purposeful life produces long-term thinking and action. Purposeful sales people promise only what can be delivered because they want to establish a relationship with their customers that will bear fruit for many years. The purposeful customer service representative labors with angry customers because she sees their need for purpose in life. She knows the anger is not directed at her, and she sees the opportunity to demonstrate the peace she enjoys from living a purposeful life.

Purpose gives you the confidence to forfeit the sale today in an effort to build a relationship forever. Purpose gives you the confidence to see the angry customer through to a happy ending. Purpose dictates actions that build trust, like making only those promises you know you can keep.

4. PROMISE AND DELIVER ONLY WHAT IS IN THE BEST INTEREST OF THE OTHER PERSON

The weight of my commitment to Darla became uncomfortably clear some years later while talking with her over the phone about a week of vacation. In the midst of that conversation, I knew what had to be done. I remembered my commitment to help her grow.

Unfortunately people sometimes put well-intended friends and coworkers in the role of the enabler. I knew Darla had a problem, and to allow her problem to escalate without confronting her made me her enabler. I had promised to do what was best for her, and now the best meant a confrontation. She was spinning out of control and did not know how to stop. Her call for a vacation was really a cry for help. Darla was relieved that I kept the implied promise of relationships of acting in the best interest of others.

Acting in Darla's best interest did not mean I confronted her and then controlled her decision, nor did it mean I abdicated the decision for treatment totally to her. Acting in another person's best interest means we empower them to discover the best choice. We do that by taking a long-term view of the relationship and loving them when they are unlovable. We act in their best interest when patience is needed but time is short.

Trust can be illustrated as a continuum.

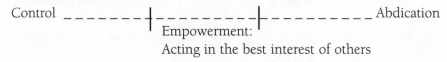

Control — — — — — — — |— — — — — — — — — |— — — — — — — Abdication
Empowerment:
Acting in the best interest of others

President Ronald Reagan, when speaking about Soviet compliance with U.S.-Soviet agreements, said he would "trust but verify." That is a great description of the promise to act in the best interest of others. Total mistrust would have led Reagan to control the Soviets through military force. Absolute, total trust would have led Reagan to abdicate his responsibility in the relationship with the Soviets by leaving the treaty signing and never thinking of the agreement again. That is trust taken to an extreme which becomes unhealthy, indeed dangerous to the Soviets, Americans, and the world. The midpoint of the trust continuum is where trust is built through a process of verification. There Reagan empowered the Soviets to live up to the agreement, and he validated that trust periodically with inspections.

My relationship with Darla could be placed on the trust continuum. I could have demonstrated total mistrust for Darla by attempting to control her decision to seek treatment. Sometimes such action is in the best interest of the other party, but that was not the case at that time with Darla. I could have taken the common position of "that is her private life" and abdicated my promise to act in her best interest. Instead I chose to demonstrate my trust by empowering her to make the best decision and seek treatment, then to confirm her trustworthiness by periodically verifying her compliance with her treatment schedule. As I verified her compliance and found her to be sober, she learned I was trustworthy by my follow-through on the promise to act in her best interest. She also learned to trust herself because my inquiries about her treatment caused her to reflect on the promise she was keeping to stay sober.

Your purpose in life will always call you to act in the best interest of the other person. Your purpose will always call you to act on a person's need and not on his or her request. Your purpose will always lead you to promise only that which you can deliver. Your purpose statement is the filter to determine the promise you make. Your purpose will always take the form of keeping your promises because promise keeping builds trust on which relationships are built. Through strong relationships, we achieve our purpose.

THE IMPORTANCE OF PURPOSE IN PRACTICE

Trust is built slowly, every day as we build a record of promise keeping. One broken promise can destroy the trust it took years of promise keeping to build. Purpose is the objective that helps us determine the promises we should make because, at the end of the day, it is our purpose that we will support with our time, energy, and finances.

More than once I have accepted a position on the board of an organization for which I had no passion. The organizations did good work, but for me their work was not best. Soon I was missing board meetings because another activity more in line with my purpose took priority. More times than not, I resigned before my term expired. My broken promise to serve on the board diminished my relationships with the others on the board.

My broken promises disrupted the consistent living of my purpose. Consistent living of our purpose is what promise keeping builds through the character equation. The results are positive, healthy relationships built on the firm foundation of trust.

APPLY THE CHARACTER EQUATION

1. What characteristics cause you to trust other people?
2. What characteristics do you possess that cause others to trust you?
3. Select five relationships from different areas of your life—home, work, etc. Now plot the level of trust in those relationships along the trust continuum.

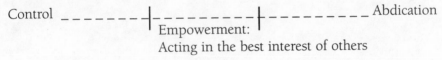

Control _ _ _ _ _ _ _ _|_ _ _ _ _ _ _ _ _|_ _ _ _ _ _ _ _ _ Abdication
                    Empowerment:
              Acting in the best interest of others

4. Based on the above, what areas of promise keeping do you need to improve? What measurable steps can you take in each area?

TWELVE

$S_2 = Stewardship$

MY DAY AT THE OFFICE

*M*ost people will arrive late to work once or twice; but when a pattern of tardiness develops, it is time to intervene. Tommy had developed such a pattern. Everyone in Tommy's area knew he was routinely fifteen to thirty minutes late for work. But when we probed a little deeper into Tommy's obvious problem, we found other problems. Tommy had also poorly managed his relationships at work by asking his coworkers to cover for him.

Tommy, like many of his coworkers, carried the Purpose Deficiency Syndrome virus. Poor stewardship is one mark of the disease. Stewardship is the practice of managing your life in the direction of your purpose. Stewards take responsibility for their lives and their decisions. Stewards tackle life looking for opportunities to develop their natural abilities, their unique passions, and their relationships. Stewards do not "hope" life will turn out all right. They make decisions to ensure it will!

Are you a steward of your purpose, or are you afflicted with Purpose Deficiency Syndrome? Purpose Deficiency Syndrome zaps a person's passion, and without passion it is hard to spring out of bed in the morning. Without passion it is difficult to bring energy to the task. Without passion it is easy to become cynical and selfish. Purpose Deficiency Syndrome-induced selfishness was Tommy's core problem.

THE NEED FOR STEWARDSHIP

In truth you are who you are becoming, and you are becoming who you are. Who you become is a process of building on who you are today and the day after and the day after and so on. Therefore, the decisions you make

95

today shape who you will be tomorrow. If you follow the pattern of most people, you will not consider your purpose and who you are becoming. Instead you follow the herd, living day to day with little to no direction. The practice of stewardship is not part of your character equation, and you are missing your intended mark in life—your purpose.

Poor stewardship shows up in the way we manage our time. Tommy did not manage his time well, but his lack of passion also contributed to his tardiness. Tommy is not alone. According to a CCH study, "Only 28% of sick leave is used for personal illness."[1] How do people use the other 72 percent of sick leave? I suspect some of the time used is due to a person's poor planning. Perhaps these poor stewards just ran out of time to handle personal issues and let their employer pay the price through sick leave. Others may call in sick because they are void of passion for their work.

Poor stewardship can be found in the way we develop our abilities. A study by the Hewitt Company found that "approximately 72% of full-time employees are eligible for their companies' job-related tuition assistance, yet only 7% take advantage of that valuable perk."[2] Why do less than 10 percent of those eligible take advantage of a free opportunity to improve their knowledge and ability? Purpose Deficiency Syndrome causes most people to say, "Why bother?"

Character requires stewardship. In practice, stewardship drives Purpose Deficiency Syndrome away because the steward engages in activities that build ability and passion and relationships. Practicing stewardship brings our purpose to life.

STEPS TO BETTER STEWARDSHIP

Maybe you are infected with Purpose Deficiency Syndrome. The practice of stewardship is a great way to start the healing process toward purposeful living. Our three steps are:

1. Understand the value of your work.
2. Develop your learning program.
3. Stop hoping and start deciding.

1. UNDERSTAND THE VALUE OF YOUR WORK

Tommy did not get it. He did not understand the greater good of his contribution to the product of the company, so he rationalized that being late was "no big deal." In fact, his tardiness *was* a big deal, especially to his coworkers who depended on him to get work out on a timely basis. We tried regularly talking about our product and its meaning in the lives of our customers. We talked about the value of satisfied customers to all members of the company team. Tommy still did not get it!

One cold January morning, I met with a representative of an organization called Christmas in April. Christmas in April organizes a community to fix and remodel dilapidated homes of needy people during the month of April. The organization, having just moved to my city, needed a corporate sponsor to help get the project kicked off. We signed on immediately because we believed in the mission and because this project provided us the opportunity to volunteer our time and skills in the area of our expertise.

All of us were excited about the project, including Tommy! On a Saturday morning in April, Tommy finally understood. He got it; and when he did, his passion could not be contained. We invested a day helping Mrs. Nelson paint and weatherproof her home. We fixed a gaping hole in her kitchen floor. When we left Mrs. Nelson that day, her home was different, and we were changed.

Monday morning Tommy was a few minutes early for work. That became his pattern. Once he understood the value of his product and the value of his place on the corporate team, he began to sense a greater good, a purpose in his work. He became a steward of his time, talent, and relationships.

Volunteerism among corporations is a growing phenomenon. "One third of large companies now have a formal policy to pay workers or give them time off for volunteer work."[3] Charles Schwab brought 900 employees to San Francisco to build houses and renovate schools in low-income neighborhoods.[4] Home Depot dispatched 150 employees to renovate a women's shelter in Long Beach, California.[5] Employees of Bank Boston spend one Saturday each month sorting food for the poor.[6]

Seeing the big picture of our lives is difficult when we are stuck in the daily frame of its demands and stresses. The Christmas in April project helped us step out of that frame and see a picture of what we could become. Studies confirm our experience: "Workers who volunteer at something they find meaningful return to work more fulfilled and motivated."[7]

2. DEVELOP YOUR LEARNING PROGRAM

This is your opportunity to develop your inborn abilities. Like muscles, abilities atrophy without exercise. Tommy's purpose button was pushed at Mrs. Nelson's home. In addition to establishing a pattern of timeliness, Tommy enrolled in training to develop his knowledge and abilities. He was amazed at all he grew to accomplish. His motivation to understand and practice his purpose grew stronger. He became the go-to guy when questions about our product or process were raised. It was no surprise who was selected when a supervisor slot opened—Tommy, of course!

3. STOP HOPING AND START DECIDING

Tommy had wandered through life, never giving much thought to the future, just hoping everything would turn out all right. While remodeling a home, his heart was rebuilt. He turned from the typical Purpose Deficiency Syndrome resignation of hoping to the purposeful practice of deciding. Tommy's passion fire was lit. He began strengthening his ability, and his relationships began to blossom. Why? Because he decided they would!

We are stewards of our relationships. We can wander through life hoping our relationships turn out all right. Or we can decide that our relationships will flourish. It is really a matter of our stewardship as this story, given to me by a friend, points out.

While waiting to pick up a friend at the airport in Portland, Oregon, I had one of those life-changing experiences that you hear other people talk about—the kind that sneaks up on you unexpectedly. This one occurred a mere two feet away from me. Straining to locate my friend among the passengers deplaning through the jetway, I noticed a man coming toward me carrying two light bags. He stopped right next to me to greet his family.

First, he motioned to his youngest son (maybe six years old) as he laid down his bags. They gave each other a long, loving hug. As they separated enough to look in each other's face, I heard the father say, "It's so good to see you, son. I missed you so much!"

His son smiled somewhat shyly, averted his eyes and replied softly, "Me, too, Dad!"

Then the man stood up, gazed in the eyes of his oldest son (maybe nine or ten), and while cupping his son's face in his hands said, "You're already quite the young man. I love you very much, Zach!" They too hugged a most loving, tender hug.

While this was happening, a baby girl (perhaps one or one and a half) was squirming excitedly in her mother's arms, never once taking her little eyes off the wonderful sight of her returning father. The man said, "Hi, baby girl!" as he gently took the child from her mother. He quickly kissed her face all over and then held her close to his chest while rocking her from side to side. The little girl instantly relaxed and simply laid her head on his shoulder, motionless in pure contentment.

After several moments, he handed his daughter to his oldest son and declared, "I've saved the best for last!" and proceeded to give his wife the longest, most passionate kiss I had seen in quite a while. He gazed into her eyes for several seconds and then silently mouthed. "I love you so much!" They gazed into each other's eyes, beaming big smiles at each other, while holding both hands.

For an instant they reminded me of newlyweds, but I knew by the age of their kids that they couldn't possibly be. I puzzled about it for a moment, then realized how totally engrossed I was in the wonderful display of unconditional love not more than an arm's length away from me.

I suddenly felt uncomfortable, as if I were invading something sacred, but was amazed to hear my own voice nervously ask, "Wow! How long have you two been married?"

"Been together fourteen years total, married twelve of those." he replied, without breaking his gaze from his lovely wife's face.

"Well then, how long have you been away?" I asked.

The man finally turned and looked at me, still beaming his joyous smile. "Two whole days!"

Two days? I was stunned. By the intensity of the greeting, I had assumed he'd been gone for at least several weeks—if not months. I know my expression betrayed me.

I said almost offhandedly, hoping to end my intrusion with some semblance of grace (and to get back to searching for my friend), "I hope my marriage is still that passionate after twelve years!"

The man suddenly stopped smiling. He looked me straight in the eye, and with forcefulness that burned right into my soul, he told me something that left me a different person. He said, "Don't hope, friend . . . decide!" Then he flashed me his wonderful smile again, shook my hand, and said, "God bless!"

With that, he and his family turned and strode away together. I was still watching that exceptional man and his special family walk just out of sight when my friend came up to me and asked, "What'cha looking at?"

Without hesitating, and with a curious sense of certainty, I replied, "My future!"

Your future is found in your purpose, and you will become your purpose only if you practice it every day. That is a decision only you can make.

THE IMPORTANCE OF PURPOSE IN PRACTICE

Stewardship is a practice that rekindles your passion, develops your abilities, and enlivens your relationships. The practice of stewardship clarifies your understanding of your purpose; and your purpose, as the organizing principle of your life, clarifies your stewardship. Your purpose reveals where to invest your time and abilities while developing purpose-driven relationships.

Stewardship, as a variable in the character equation, increases your ability to serve and helps you find balance in your life. The decision to be a steward of your purpose builds character!

APPLY THE CHARACTER EQUATION

1. List volunteer opportunities in your community that interest you.
2. Which of these opportunities exercise your work-related expertise? Volunteer today.
3. List the training opportunities offered in your workplace. In which of these opportunities will you enroll?
4. How can you be a better steward of your relationships at work and at home?

THIRTEEN

$\mathcal{I} = Integrity$

MY DAY AT THE OFFICE

*A*t 2:15 P.M. on that day in my office, Iris confidently proposed switching from our current microfilm system to an electronic imaging system because imaging was more efficient. With imaging, an unlimited number of our people could work on a document at the same time. Under our current system the actual note had to be passed from one area to another, making it available to only one person at a time. The number of people required to do the work significantly decreased with the imaging system. In fact, the new imaging system required a manager with skills and knowledge Iris did not have. By proposing imaging, Iris actually put her job at risk.

What are you willing to do to keep your job? Most people in Iris's position and with her skills set would not have brought imaging to my attention. But most people, 80 percent according to Wilson Learning, are wandering through life infected with Purpose Deficiency Syndrome. Most people think in terms of, *What must I do to keep my job?* That question reveals a Purpose Deficiency Syndrome-driven perspective.

The correct question each of us must ask is this, "What must I do to achieve my purpose?" That was the question Iris asked herself, and her integrity compelled the meeting with me. Integrity means practicing my purpose regardless of the circumstances or consequences. It is important to remember that a person's true purpose in life will always be honorable and will always work together with the purposes of others for everyone's long-term, indeed eternal, benefit. A person who claims a purpose less than that is rationalizing the fulfillment of a selfish desire.

Selfish desire is the enemy of character. A self-centered, Purpose Deficiency Syndrome perspective causes people to rationalize behavior that is harmful to others and themselves. The perspective of a purposeful life is focused on our purpose rather than ourselves. Integrity becomes a measurement of how consistently our practice matches our purpose.

THE NEED FOR INTEGRITY

Integrity in the context of the character equation of many people measures quite low. Just read the headlines of the morning paper. As I write this book, President Clinton is attempting to redefine *sexual relations* to justify his behavior. Some of President Clinton's political adversaries are adding to the scandal by using his breach of integrity for their own political gain.

When the CEO of the United States, the leader of the free world, lowers his standard of practice, it is not surprising that others have and continue to do the same. Ripped from the headlines:

- "Hospitals Profit by 'Upcoding' Illnesses"—Medicare pays hospitals for the service provided Medicare patients based on a system called, "Diagnosis Related Groups," or "DRG." According to an article in the *Wall Street Journal,* "Upcoding—the practice of upgrading the seriousness of a medical malady by filing Medicare bills under the DRG code that will carry the highest price—appears to be an epidemic in the industry." Upcoding pays big bucks! DRG #143 for "Chest Pain" pays $2,089, but upcoding to DRG #129 for "Cardiac Arrest, unexplained" increases the pay to $4,526. DRG #90 for "Simple Pneumonia" pays $2,791, but upcoding to DRG #89 for "Pneumonia, complications" pays $4,462. DRG #155 for "Bleeding Ulcer" pays $5,624, but upcoding to DRG #154 for "Bleeding Ulcer, complications" pays $16,726. Fudging just a little seems to pay an awful lot. The Department of Health and Human Services advised hospitals, "Don't upcode—bill for what you do and do what you bill for." In spite of this advice, some hospitals have employed consultants to teach upcoding to employees and pay the consultants a percentage of the increased revenue.[1]
- "Tobacco firm memo: 'Bury' unfavorable research—Memo's revealing deception and deceit emerged in the midst of litigation against the tobacco industry. "One, a November 1977 memo about a researcher's efforts, written by Phillip Morris scientist William Dunn, suggests a cover up should the results prove damaging about nicotine's effects. 'If she is able to demonstrate, as she anticipates, no withdrawal effects of nicotine, we will want to pursue this avenue with some vigor. If, how-

ever, the results with nicotine are similar to those gotten with morphine and caffeine, we will want to bury it,' Dunn wrote."[2]

Breaches of integrity become an institutional problem when its individual members fail at the practice of life. "Forty-five percent of workers say they have committed at least one of a dozen actions over a twelve-month period that are either unethical or fall into a gray area," according to a study sponsored by the American Society of Chartered Life Underwriters and Chartered Financial Consultants and the Ethics Officers Association. Cases included, among others, using company property to search for another job and sabotaging company data.[3]

An earlier study sponsored by the same organizations found approximately 48 percent of the workforce admitted to one or more unethical behaviors, including cutting corners on quality, lying to customers and supervisors, and having an affair with a business associate.[4]

Our world has a desperate need for purposeful people to live with integrity. The majority of people are wandering through life hoping for that one-in-ten-million sweepstakes prize. In fact, James Patterson and Peter Kim in their book *The Day America Told the Truth*, asked, "What are you willing to do for $10 million?" Two out of three respondents agreed to at least one of the following, some to several:

- Would abandon their entire family
- Would abandon their church
- Would become prostitutes for a week or more
- Would give up their American citizenship
- Would leave their spouses
- Would withhold testimony and let a murderer go free
- Would kill a stranger
- Would change their race
- Would have a sex-change operation
- Would put their children up for adoption[5]

When the president of the United States puts self-gratification ahead of his purpose, it is time for ordinary, everyday people of character to lead through practicing life with integrity. When major businesses trade integrity for profit, it is time for ordinary, everyday people of character to lead through practicing life with integrity. When two-thirds of Americans are willing to sell their children, spouses, families, citizenship, and dignity, it is time for ordinary, everyday people of character to lead through practicing life with integrity.

STEPS TO LIFE WITH INTEGRITY

You are the ordinary, everyday people of character, and the challenge is yours to raise the standard practice of your life. Integrity can be developed and improved through three steps:

1. Run a different race.
2. Get on a compatible team.
3. Establish a goal of blamelessness.

1. RUN A DIFFERENT RACE

You live and work with people every day who look like you, dress like you, live in similar houses (with similar payments), and drive comparable cars (with comparable payments). You and these people appear to be living similar lives; but if you are attempting to live a purposeful, character-filled life, you are running in a different race!

Some of the people behind the stories mentioned in this chapter are suffering from Purpose Deficiency Syndrome. They have not given a moment's thought to purpose and how it might impact their future. They are living for the comfort of today. Iris was and is running a different race. She is less concerned about short-term circumstances and more concerned about how her practice of life in the short-term will impact her purpose in the long-term.

Know your purpose, and then focus on practicing your purpose every day. Living and practicing a purposeful life is a different paradigm; it is a different race. Along the way you may find that others, especially those with Purpose Deficiency Syndrome, are getting ahead of you, but you must not succumb to that germ of Purpose Deficiency Syndrome thinking. Just remember, you are running a different race!

2. GET ON A COMPATIBLE TEAM

This point has been made, but its importance requires one more mention. You cannot achieve your purpose alone. For that reason, relationships are a major part of the purpose equation. Surrounding yourself with like-minded, purposeful people increases the likelihood you will achieve your purpose. The old saying goes, "If you lie down with dogs, you are going to get fleas." Paul said it well, "Do not be misled: 'Bad company corrupts good character'" (1 Cor. 15:33).

You may be looking for a job now. Instead of wondering if some company is going to hire you, consider if you are willing to hire them to be your employer. Instead of the job interview being a forum where they can ask you questions, go prepared to ask them questions. Find out if the prospective employer and its people are purposeful people of character.

You may be employed but feel you are on the wrong team. Perhaps your coworkers have crossed the line of integrity. If so, you have two choices. You can change the team, or you can get off the team. Stephanie Stephenson yearned for her chance on the Broadway stage. When the call came, Stephanie was offered a role in *Les Miserables*! One day after landing her choice role, she quit when she learned she would have to play a prostitute who was groped and actually touched. Stephanie was offered the break she had dreamed about, but it was a role on the wrong team, so she quit.

James Spann is another purposeful person who practices life with integrity. Spann is a weatherman in Birmingham, Alabama. When the station where Spann was working changed hands, the new owners changed its affiliation from NBC to Fox. Spann did not agree with Fox's programming philosophy, so he left the station not knowing where he would go! That is practicing your purpose with integrity.

The point is simple: Surround yourself with people who share your desire for living a purposeful life. Find people who will hold you accountable and who will allow you to hold them accountable. Running the race with purposeful people of character is more enjoyable and achievable.

3. Establish a Goal of Blamelessness

I was advised once that "touching someone with a pat on the shoulder" was not possible any more due to the litigious nature of our society. I always thought that comment was interesting; and while seeing an explosion of litigation, I never really felt the comment was accurate. I had always expressed my interest in others through a friendly pat on the back or a quick hug and never did one person, man or woman, feel I was out of line. My friend offering the advice had a different experience. In his case, people did take exception to his gesture, and some even lodged complaints.

Why did my friend and I have such different experiences? I learned the answer to that question through experience, and it can be summed up in one word—blamelessness. The original word for *blameless* can be traced back to a Hebrew word meaning "perfectly pure in heart." My friend could not pat someone on the back, and he certainly could not give someone a hug, because he failed the test of blamelessness in the eyes of his coworkers. He had a long, sordid history of affairs. He was known to use his position to persuade young female associates to engage in sexual relationships. So, when he touched a woman at work, even with honorable motives, he was not blameless. If a coworker alleged you had sexually harassed her, how would the others you know best react? Would they wonder if the allegation were true, or would they know that the allegation could not possibly be true? Blamelessness is when the people we know best know such an allegation could not be true. They laugh at the charge.

Blamelessness is earned as we practice our purpose. We are blameless because we have established a pattern of integrity. People trust us because they know we trust our purpose. What gave Iris the courage to bring imaging to my attention? Iris trusted her purpose. Experience had taught Iris that following her purpose always landed her in a better place. Certainly Iris had experienced difficulty along the way; but looking back, each experience had been used to bring her to her current position. Showing me a better way to accomplish her work was consistent with her calling; and if that meant she would be forced to find another job, she knew it was for the best. That perspective is the result of a pure, blameless heart, practicing life with integrity. As you might suspect, purposeful people like Iris who practice life with such integrity are hard to find. Iris was promoted!

Aaron Feuerstein understands blamelessness. He is the owner of Malden Mills, a manufacturing business in northern Massachusetts. When fire destroyed his plant, most of his workers thought he would take the insurance money and walk away, but he did not. In fact, a week after the fire, Feuerstein announced he was keeping all employees on the payroll for one month. One month turned into two months. Two months became three. Everyone was astonished. Many people would have walked away, but Feuerstein had a purpose, and that purpose could be served by sitting on the sidelines. So he did an uncommon thing by continuing to pay his people while they were out of work waiting for the plant to be rebuilt.[6]

Blamelessness results when we consistently practice our purpose through sacrificial acts like risking our job to stay true to our purpose and continuing to make payroll even though the business is shut down!

THE IMPORTANCE OF PURPOSE IN PRACTICE

Socrates said, "The key to greatness is to be in reality who we say we are." If we claim to be a person of character and purpose, we must demonstrate the integrity to show it. Our public life should match our private life. Our behavior should match our belief. Our reaction should match our rhetoric. Integrity is rare today in part because too few people have really defined their purpose; and until you define your purpose, you cannot practice it consistently. Consistently practicing our purpose is difficult even when we understand it. Integrity always rewards the purposeful by affirming the purpose, building credibility among peers, creating opportunities for leadership, deepening your passion, and developing strong relationships.

APPLY THE CHARACTER EQUATION
1. In what ways do you keep your purpose in focus?
2. Do you consistently practice your purpose? What changes do you need to make to practice life with integrity?

Applying the Character Equation

The character equation teaches that purpose and practice are linked. Purpose leads to practice, and practice leads to purpose. Further, each variable of the character equation affects the other. One variable may overlap the other as it extends to the next. For example, the variable "expressed value" is an action taken in the life of another. "Communication" is another variable that affects the way we express value. "Integrity" builds the credibility to be heard.

The character equation is useless if it is not applied in your life. This section applies the character equation to six real-life issues you face.

Fourteen

Difficult People

*A*ngela Story's department of her midwestern employer, an advertising agency, is full of character—well, actually, characters. Taking a project from concept to design to completion requires a diverse team of individuals, and Angela's department is certainly a group of individuals.

James is the team's thought leader. He leads the team's contact with their client and has responsibility for generating the core message that will achieve the client's desired results. Albert is the writer of the group. He translates James's message into words. Lucy is the team's copy editor. She reviews Albert's work, making any necessary grammatical changes and offering her insight on his wordsmithery. Scarlet is the graphic artist. She translates James's message into visual image. Angela is the team's media buyer, spending her days investing her client's money in the most impacting combination of television, radio, print, and Internet exposure.

The individual team members are interdependent on one another. James's message means little if Albert and Scarlet cannot communicate it effectively and if Lucy misses grammatical and thematic problems in the copy. All the work of the team amounts to little should Angela place the final product in the wrong place or at the wrong time. The team must function together to create a product and serve the needs of their client.

Well-oiled is a term often used to describe a team that functions well together. *Well-oiled* is not a term that describes Angela's team most days. The average day around their office finds James meeting with other members of the team, soliciting their input regarding their client's message. These meetings are becoming increasingly strained. It seems his team members are not as forthcoming as before.

Around the corner Albert and Lucy are at war over his choice of words. It seems James is quite perturbed that Lucy is suggesting an alternative approach to his handiwork. James is feeling that Lucy is becoming increasingly difficult. Lucy believes it is her duty to suggest alternative approaches to those advocated by James. Scarlet, the artist, is rarely on time with her work; but when the message is finally printed, she makes sure the entire team is made aware by ringing a bell. Annoyed by her tardiness, the team has stopped running to her cubicle to "ooh and aah" over her masterpiece. Angela avoids conflict, which is arising often; and she is beginning to keep her distance from the rest of the team.

Angela works with a cast of difficult characters, all of whom have relatives in most workplaces. Can you identify these characters where you work?

- 007—This is the office double agent. These people are engaging as they ask your opinion about a subject. The best double agents make you feel like you are the most important, most intelligent person on earth. They pick your brain and inventory your good ideas. Suddenly a memo crosses your desk, informing you of a direction, or new product, or new campaign and praising the originator of this great idea— the double agent. The double agent's great idea sounds frighteningly like the idea you gave the double agent only a few days ago. The double agent is disguised as your friend as long as you are forthcoming with information—until you catch on to the game. James is the office 007.

- Einstein—This is the office know-it-all. Einsteins are obsessed with being right. These people are instant experts on everything. Just when everyone seems to be getting along well and the entire team is engaged in the conversation, Einstein voices his "knowledge" of the topic, revealing his ignorance and feelings of self-importance. The conversation ends, and tension permeates the office. Albert is the office Einstein.

- Lucifer—This is the office "devil's advocate." These are the people who appear to block every good idea with a "yes, but" and "I have another idea." Malicious Lucifers enjoy setting you up to make a suggestion so they can shoot you down. Lucifers see their role as a calling and never miss an opportunity to tell you why an idea will not work. Lucy is the office Lucifer.

- O'Hara—This is the office "star," the center of attention. O'Haras demand center stage; and if you do not accommodate their unquenchable thirst for the limelight, they will create circumstances that call attention to themselves. It does not matter to an O'Hara if the circumstances are good or bad as long as the eyes of their coworkers are firmly fixed on them. O'Haras will be loud and boisterous. They will pout and whine. They will make sure the team acknowledges their good work. Scarlet is this office's O'Hara.

- Aunt Bea—This is the office enabler. The Aunt Beas run from conflict. The more unpleasant the work environment the more withdrawn these people become, allowing the other characters the unchecked freedom to continue their difficult ways. Angela is the Aunt Bea of this office.

The causes of Angela's office meltdown become clear once you understand these challenging characters. James's teammates are becoming less forthcoming because all of their ideas are showing up as his work. His coworkers want and deserve public acknowledgment of their contribution; but James, the 007 double agent, is sworn to secrecy. Albert, the office Einstein, cannot abide Lucy, the devil's advocate, questioning his wisdom and offering alternative suggestions. Lucy believes her objectivity is a gift to be used in all situations. Scarlet O'Hara rings the bell signaling the team to come running. If the bell fails, Scarlet posts her masterpiece in the break room where she takes conspicuously long breaks until she and her work have encumbered the entire team. Aunt Bea, better known to her coworkers as Angela, stays on task, telling herself things will get better. Meanwhile the meltdown continues, her coworkers become increasingly difficult, and Angela becomes increasingly unhappy.

Difficult people and the inherent conflict of their behavior are present in workplaces everywhere. In 1986, an estimated 9 percent of management's time was spent resolving personality conflicts. By 1996, that estimate doubled to 18 percent.[1] Difficult people and their personality clashes, such as in Angela's office, are only part of the reason more time and money are spent resolving conflict. Other conflict catalysts include:

- A workforce unskilled in the practice of communication
- Failure of management to delineate clearly the lines of authority
- People spending more time on the job rubbing against other difficult personalities
- Downsizing, which leaves the same amount of work to be spread over fewer people
- People having no real purpose that leads to a selfless practice of life

Work and life can be agonizing when conflict results from the mixture of all of these catalysts together with our difficult personalities. Conflict yields agony. Our modern-day English word *agony* is derived from the ancient Greek word for *conflict, agon*. Conflict yields agony when there is little or no hope that a difficult situation will get better. Conflict yields agony in the workplace when difficult personalities mix with other catalysts, resulting in a hopeless and torturous daily operating environment.

Agony engulfs us when we lose hope of changing the meltdown, the downward-spiraling, torturous daily operating environment. Maybe we lose hope because we have adopted the wrong perspective. Perhaps we have grown weary seeking to change the difficult people around us only to learn we cannot change them at all. We can change only ourselves, our attitudes, our choices, and our actions. Hope is restored when we focus on ourselves and begin to experience change.

The character equation is an investment in personal change and growth, placing emphasis on personal responsibility instead of spending time and energy in futile attempts to change others. The character equation helps difficult people become more tolerable, and conflict more manageable.

THE CHARACTER EQUATION

PURPOSE

Difficult people bring conflict because they are not at peace with themselves. They are themselves conflicted. Internal conflict feels like an eternal, gnawing pain in your gut; and enduring such ever-present pain inevitably leads its victims to try whatever means necessary to wipe it out.

Some difficult people feel achievement will satisfy their pain. Like James, these difficult people co-opt good ideas and pass them off as their work because their internal conflict results in their not believing their ideas are good enough.

Some difficult people feel being one step ahead or above another person will satisfy their pain. Albert uses his intellect as a tool for staying on top. He wants people to affirm his intelligence to ensure that he is still ahead or on top of the pack.

Some people attempt to satisfy their pain by not allowing others to feel good about themselves. Lucy plays that role. She plays the devil's advocate to call into question the performance of another. Lucy's devil's advocacy goes well beyond periodic objective questioning which can be helpful. Instead, Lucy uses the skill to transfer her pain to others.

Some people feel recognition is the cure for their pain and, like Scarlet, they seek it everywhere. These people, feeling no internal sense of worth, see recognition as an affirmation of their value. So by whatever means, good or bad, they gain the spotlight.

Some people try to satisfy their pain through others' approval. These people, like Angela, suppress their internal pain, avoid conflict with others, and spend their energy trying to please everyone. Angela, however, will never resolve her own pain trying to please a group of conflicted, difficult people who cannot be pleased.

The source of internal conflict and pain is purpose deficiency. Our cast of characters—James, Albert, Lucy, Scarlet, and Angela—have probably not taken an inventory of their unique abilities and directed those abilities toward the purpose of their lives. Understanding purpose resolves internal conflict and instills confidence in our everyday decisions and ideas. Understanding purpose eliminates the double agent, the know-it-all, the devil's advocate, the star of the show, and the enabler.

If you identify with one or more of our characters, an appropriate strategy for resolving conflict is to invest in understanding your purpose. Go back to the section on purpose at the beginning of this book.

Perhaps you work with one of these characters. Leading them to discuss purpose is an appropriate strategy for dealing with the difficult people in your life. You can begin that process by understanding that internal conflict and pain arising from no sense of purpose is the root cause of their difficult personalities. People, especially difficult people, recognize in others the fulfillment, stability, and meaning that purpose gives, and they want it! Be prepared to share with them how you have found purpose in your life.

EXPRESSED VALUE

Everyone has value, even the difficult people. Especially the difficult people. Characteristics that make people difficult in relationships serve the same people well in other areas such as meeting performance standards. Scarlet's penchant for the spotlight can be annoying, but her outgoing nature is important to the client relationship. Lucy's objective questioning often crosses the line, but her ability to ask the tough questions helps the team fine-tune their message. Albert's obsession with being right can repel his coworkers, but that same obsession compels James day after day to double-check, even triple-check his assumptions about the message. Angela's desire for harmony causes her to be wishy-washy at times, and that can be frustrating. Her desire for harmony, however, brings feeling and warmth to the workplace.

The liabilities that cause people to be difficult in relationships can at the same time be assets in other areas of life. One strategy for dealing with difficult people and their conflict is to affirm the often-annoying characteristic when used as an asset.

LEARNING

Difficult people are good teachers. They teach us what not to do! Your coworker James steals your idea and you exclaim, "I will never do that to someone!" Another coworker, Albert, defiantly defends his opinion which is obviously wrong. He will not admit a better idea has emerged and you think: *He is being so pigheaded. I will never do that!* Scarlet, the star of your office, calls attention to an insignificant detail of her work, hoping to be recognized. You say to yourself: "This is sad. I will never do that!" In one of her moods, Lucy relentlessly questions Albert about his message. Tension fills the room, and you say to Angela: "Lucy has got to let go of this. I will never do that!"

In a world looking for role models, difficult people can be reverse role models. By their actions we learn what not to do. Instead of blowing off difficult persons and the conflict they create, take the opportunity to learn. Learn what not to do and commit not to do it.

COMMUNICATION

Lucy steps in your office and fires a verbal assault on your work. Albert demonstrates his know-it-all attitude. How should you respond? Solomon expressed this wisdom, "A gentle answer turns away wrath, but a harsh word stirs up anger" (Prov. 15:1). Watch your response lest you too become difficult.

This strategy for communicating with difficult people—a gentle answer—is a truthful answer communicated in a winsome way. In the midst of heated, emotional conversations, I have applied Solomon's wisdom with remarkable results. Once I was listening to a former boss screaming about some problem in the business. He was looking for a response from me—a response in kind—but I applied a gentle answer. The louder his voice, the softer my voice. His tirade ended with him bending over his desk to hear my comments. That is an example of a gentle answer using tone of voice.

Softening your tone of voice diffuses a highly emotional confrontation. Once the emotion is out of the conversation, another aspect of a "gentle" answer can be applied—speaking the truth. My boss was ready to hear my perspective calmly and objectively. He could handle the facts, the truth, and make an informed judgment.

Conveying the facts, the truth, is another strategy for communicating with difficult people. The truth disarms a difficult person. Truth has a way of clarifying a murky, conflicted situation. Difficult people can argue with you and your impressions, but they cannot argue with the truth. Always communicate the gentle answer of truth.

Solomon not only spoke proactively of how we should communicate with difficult people, but he also warned against an improper response. "A harsh word" is responding to the difficult person's attack in kind. "A harsh word" is the same word the difficult person threw in your direction. Whether used in kind or as an unexpected attack, a harsh word defines its user as a difficult person. A gentle answer is preferred, lest we become the difficult person!

Finding common ground is another strategy when dealing with some difficult people. Go to the Lucy in your workplace and ask her opinion of your work before she sees it in a meeting and begins her tireless probe. By asking her opinion, you affirm her value and benefit from her insight. You also give her ownership of your work, which in a meeting puts her in a position of questioning herself instead of you.

INTEGRITY

Ask James why he plays the role of the difficult double agent, and he would tell you, "My parents trained me not to trust anyone." In James's view, his difficult behavior is not his fault. Ask Albert why he creates conflict and difficulty as the office know-it-all, and he would tell you, "In high school the other kids called me stupid." In Albert's view his difficult personality is the product of his high school classmates. Ask Lucy why she obsessively plays the devil's advocate, and she would say, "When I was a child, my parents severely punished me for my bad decisions and said nothing about my good decisions. I learned it was better to do nothing than to risk making a bad decision." In Lucy's mind her difficult behavior is the product of her parents.

A person of character must practice integrity, which demands we stop blaming others and instead take responsibility for our difficult behavior. The truth demands that we acknowledge our own difficult behavior and change it before spending a minute considering how we can change others.

Perhaps you winced as our team members were described. Maybe you see a little bit of James or Lucy in yourself. You may have had a difficult childhood, but you do not have to remain its victim. The first step in overcoming difficult, conflict-causing behavior is to acknowledge your actions and commit to change.

DIFFICULT PEOPLE AND THE CHARACTER EQUATION

1. Identify the difficult people in your world and how these people are difficult.
2. List a positive quality for each person on your list.
3. List one way their difficult characteristic can be used in a positive way.
4. List ways you can improve communication with these difficult people.

FIFTEEN

Anger

"*G*oing postal." The saying was inspired by the high-profile, anger-induced attacks of former post office employees on their former coworkers. Today that saying is heard daily in workplaces everywhere when describing a person's angry outburst. Anger overflows in many ways, ranging from harsh words impulsively spoken to sabotaging the company computer to physical attacks on coworkers.

Anger surfaces easily in tough times. A personal or corporate crisis can push our anger from the suppressed area in the back of our minds to the visible action of our behavior. Being "right-sized" out of our job can cause us to "go postal" without warning. A major mistake can escalate stress levels, and anger is the handy response.

What about anger in good times? Isn't it logical that anger is a product of tough times and, therefore, not a factor when the good times roll? Not so, according to Bill DeFoore, author of *Anger: Deal with It, Heal It, Stop It from Killing You*. DeFoore said, "Work conditions in some ways are better than ever, but people's tolerance for unmet needs is lower, and frustration and anger and the willingness to express it is on the rise."[1] DeFoore's assertion is confirmed by a WorkForce/E.Span study which found "eighty-four percent of HR professionals said their firms were experiencing increased hostility."[2] This increased hostility is being seen in what many people consider not only the good times but also the best of times!

CAUSES OF ANGER IN YOUR WORKPLACE

PERSONAL PROBLEMS

One hard day in the office, Leah asked that she be given an extra break every afternoon because her pregnancy was at risk. Later that same day, five of her coworkers showed up to complain. Why would they object? Because Leah had been hostile to them for several years. And why had she been hostile? Because she had been infertile. Leah's infertility problem had caused her great pain and she relieved that pain every day by mistreating her coworkers.

All of us bear a painful, stressful burden, and sometimes each of us attempts to relieve the pain by releasing anger. Often our anger is directed toward people who have nothing to do with the cause of the pain. Such was the case with Leah. Leah's story is typical of situations in virtually every workplace.

UNMET EXPECTATIONS

John and Janet bought their dream vacation package with funds they had saved for seven years specifically for this trip. The pictures of the Hawaiian Islands sent to them by the travel agent were beautiful. The hotel looked great, especially the view of the ocean. For months the couple anticipated and planned the trip.

Visions of beautiful Hawaii danced in their minds as they made the long trip from Atlanta. Those glorious visions were obscured when they arrived at the hotel. Once on the property John and Janet could tell the pictures did not accurately represent the hotel. Only one room had a view of the ocean, and it was only a glimpse. The lavish meals promised were nothing more than hors d'oeuvres. Their dream vacation turned out to be a nightmare.

All of us have experienced the frustration of unmet expectations. Whether we are the customer—as in this case with John and Janet—or we are a coworker, unmet expectations often cause us to become angry.

A MEAN STREAK

Randy was recruited for a position of great responsibility. During the interview process, company officials rolled out the red carpet. Randy was offered a generous financial package. He and his wife were thrilled by the opportunity. About two months into his new work, Randy began to notice a marked difference between the man that rolled out the red carpet during the interview and the man he now worked for. Instead of rolling out the red carpet, this same man was now calling Randy "on the carpet."

Randy's red-faced, veins-popping boss would make an issue out of Randy's obvious devotion to his family. One of Randy's morning routines was to take his kids to school. Even though Randy arrived at work before the workday began, his boss objected. Lunchtime with the kids became a problem between Randy and his boss as well.

Randy could not understand why his actions were so upsetting to his boss, especially since his boss could not give Randy a reasonable explanation. Time and counsel helped Randy and his boss understand that the boss's mean streak was the result of suppressed anger. The boss was taking out his anger on Randy from circumstances unrelated to their work.

INATTENTION

I was traveling home and connecting through Atlanta's Hartsfield International Airport. The connection was tight, but my airline had assured me they would hold the flight. I sprinted from my arrival concourse to the departure concourse; and upon arrival at the departure gate, I encountered two gate agents who were busily shuffling papers.

"Hi, I am Bill Nix. I believe you are waiting on me," I said, trying to get the pair's attention.

Neither agent looked up, but one said simply, "Your flight is gone." I protested saying, "I am just two minutes late, and you said you would hold the flight!" The agents still did not look at me and continued to insist the flight was gone.

Somewhat annoyed by their obvious lack of interest in my situation, I continued, "How do you know it is gone? I have boarded many planes and sat at the gate for awhile before departing."

While running to the window, hoping to see the plane, I glanced back at the agents, hoping to get their attention; but the pair never looked my way. Though I am not proud of it, I must admit I allowed my anger to overflow at that moment, and I swiftly kicked a nearby chair. Finally, the two agents looked at me and laughed.

The people in these stories may have legitimate reasons for becoming angry. Infertility is tough on everyone who has experienced it. Hostile treatment by others almost always engenders a like response. Anger often replaces your dreams when they are dashed. A tough childhood and family life certainly leave their victims feeling cheated. Being the object of blame for just about anything and everything is frustrating. Staying on the road one more night because of a gate agent's inattention to detail boils the blood of the road warrior.

Anger arising from the circumstances of these stories is understandable and legitimate, but the legitimacy of our anger is not the point. The point is how we handle our anger so we can move past the circumstances.

THE CHARACTER EQUATION

Most of us relieve our anger in one of three ways:

1. Aggressively attacking the cause of the anger verbally or physically
2. Suppressing our anger by making ourselves believe it does not exist
3. Passive-aggressive behavior aimed at hurting the cause of our anger without drawing attention to ourselves

These three common ways of handling anger relieve our pain for a brief period but not for long. Applying one of these coping methods to our anger is like applying a Band-Aid laced with a strep infection to an open wound. The root problem of anger will not heal, and in many cases the anger only gets worse.

The character equation is not a Band-Aid. Rather, the character equation is a method that, when consistently applied, brings healing. You have the choice to apply the character equation and find healing or to follow the destructive path of anger. Several elements of the character equation can be applied to the problem of anger.

PURPOSE

The natural human spirit cries out for respect and validation because these confirm our significance. Looking solely to others and the activity of our lives for respect and validation, however, is a classic symptom of Purpose Deficiency Syndrome. The emotion of anger explodes in us when we fail to receive from others the respect and validation we seek. The activity of our lives can change in the blink of an eye, and with it goes our feeling of significance.

We become angry when our significance is threatened. Leah's sense of significance was bound up in her ability to become pregnant. Her infertility left her feeling insignificant and angry. Her anger was directed toward her coworkers, which left the group feeling disrespected, and, therefore, feeling insignificant in Leah's eyes. Leah was angry about her infertility, and her coworkers were angry at Leah. The cycle of angry pain continued when Leah's coworkers attempted to deny her a medical benefit.

John and Janet felt violated when their expectations were not met. John and Janet's anger screamed, "You cannot do this to us! You must respect us enough to tell us the truth. We are significant!" John and Janet were preserving their significance through anger.

His boss's anger had little to do with Randy, but on many days that knowledge was not enough to calm his own desire for external significance.

Like John and Janet, Randy's anger would overflow, delivering the message, "You cannot do this to me because I am significant!"

Through his angry outbursts, Randy's boss was sending his own message: "I have not experienced significance, and neither are you!" The boss knew he had blown his life if Randy could find significance. If Randy could balance the demands of his job and home, then he would have succeeded where his boss had failed. As Randy's sense of significance grew, the boss's sense of failure in his own life grew.

When the gate agents did not even look me in the eye, I became enraged. Around and around in my mind this question flew ever faster, "How could they let that plane go and not respect me enough to break their stride to explain? Don't these guys know how much I fly this airline?" Eventually I allowed my anger to cause me to behave in a childish way.

Like all of the people highlighted in this chapter, I sought significance in the eyes of others. True significance, however, comes from a well-defined sense of purpose. We experience significance when we apply our purpose in the lives of others, not from how others treat us.

The character equation reminds us to focus on purpose. A focus on purpose bottles the energy we gain from the emotion of anger and sends it in a healthy direction. Understanding our unique abilities and our passions helps us keep "focused on our priorities—our purpose." When I settled down a few minutes after attacking the innocent but convenient airport furniture, I realized that missing a flight was a small event in the context of my significant, purposeful life. If Leah's coworkers had focused on their purposes, they would have responded to Leah's early hostility by helping her. A healthy sense of purpose would have led John and Janet to acknowledge their disappointment and point out the false advertisement to the hotel manager, but they would not have allowed the disappointment to ruin their dream trip. A keen sense of purpose would have taught Randy's boss that in spite of his past he could enjoy a significant future.

Purpose brings the perspective of objective, innate significance that does not depend on anyone for validation. Purpose frees us to master our emotions, even the powerful and prevalent emotion of anger.

EXPRESSED VALUE

Expressing value is an effective anger prevention and anger management tool. When expressing value for another person, your focus is on that person's needs, not your own needs. It is rather difficult to become angry with people when you are serving them.

Leah's coworkers missed an unusual opportunity to express value in her life. Instead of focusing on why Leah was so difficult to work with, this gang of five gave in to their purpose deficiency and focused inward. These women were more concerned about how Leah treated them than they were about how they treated Leah.

One simple expression of value would have broken the fragile wall around Leah's emotion. One touch on her shoulder coupled with a word of concern would have melted Leah's aching heart. One invitation to lunch with the other women would have opened the doorway through which Leah was not invited. The episode with Leah and the women could have been prevented by an investment of simple expressions of value.

Expressing value is not only a tool to prevent anger but also a tool to manage anger. Though we try, sometimes we fail to prevent a circumstance that results in an explosion of anger. Randy was not the cause of his boss's anger, just its target. At first Randy was confused by his boss's actions, but in time he learned his boss's outbursts were the result of pain from long ago.

Randy knew he could not control or prevent his boss's anger, so he learned to manage it. His simple technique was to reinforce his boss's positive acts and play those scenes in his mind when his boss was inappropriately angry. When his boss acted kindly toward someone, Randy would record the act in a journal and, when appropriate, compliment his boss for his kindness. When the boss lost his cool, Randy could retreat to the journal and be reminded of the good his boss had done. It was his boss's previous expressions of value that guided Randy in the midst of his boss's expressions of anger.

LEARNING

Applying the practice of learning is simple, "Bear with each other and forgive whatever grievances you may have against one another" (Col. 3:13). How much of our anger could be avoided if we heeded this wisdom? But for forgiveness to be effective, all the angry parties must be in agreement. Leah and her coworkers finally developed a positive relationship but not until all of them acknowledged their faults and asked the others for forgiveness.

Certainly one party can offer forgiveness, and that offer is therapeutic for the giver; but for forgiveness to have its greatest impact, all affected parties must participate. Leah could have forgiven the women, and she would have been the better for it; but their relationship could not turn positive until the five women followed Leah's lead.

Learning often requires that we clear the air with forgiveness. Once cleansed of the anger of the past, we are free and clear minded to pursue our purpose.

BALANCE

Inappropriate expressions of anger are sometimes the result of our loss of objectivity. Our thinking gets skewed. We become paranoid, believing everyone is our enemy. Then our behavior matches our belief. We allow our anger to rule our action.

Perhaps our running has left us exhausted. Maybe we are failing in our work. Too often we neglect our spiritual and emotional needs. Some of us are simply out of shape physically. Whatever the reason we are out of balance, the result is the same—an inability to think and act objectively.

I was physically exhausted the evening I kicked the airport chair. Not only was I tired from a week of travel, but I was also worn out from a bag-laden sprint from the terminal to the gate. *Objective* would not have been a word the gate agents might have used to describe me; but after a few minutes and a conversation with my ever-understanding wife, Teri, I realized my plight was not that desperate. There was another flight ninety minutes later, and I was on it.

Losing my cool with the gate agents was inevitable because I was so out of balance at that moment. My response might have been more positive had I been living a balanced life. A balanced perspective cannot be mustered in the heat of the moment. Balance requires daily effort.

ACCOUNTABILITY

Randy's boss knew he had a problem with anger. In fact, he talked with Randy about his problem several times; and each time Randy suggested he partner with a trusted friend for the purpose of accountability. Wisely, the boss listened to Randy and entered into such a relationship with an old friend. Each week Randy's boss and his friend met and discussed the boss's feelings and actions. Randy's boss, serious about change, opened up to his friend, sharing experiences, thoughts, and fears he had not shared with anyone before. The vulnerability of that relationship and the purging of a painful past served as a change agent for Randy's boss. The distance between angry outbursts grew. In time, Randy's boss enjoyed a new reputation for level-headed, measured response.

All of us need accountability. Like Randy's boss, we all have areas of weakness that will grow unless we find ways to change. Our purpose ultimately relates to meeting the needs of people. One of those needs common to all people is the need for accountability.

COMMUNICATION

Words are important. In the midst of a fit of anger, words often destroy like a cruise missile. Randy and many of his coworkers experienced the devastation of their boss's incoming verbal attacks.

Communicating with words that heal in the midst of anger is an act of our will. Most of us would rather return a verbal missile with an even stronger barrage of word-fire. But healing is necessary to rebuild after anger destroys us. Just as words can tear us apart, words can put us back together. Solomon wrote, "Reckless words pierce like a sword, but the tongue of the wise brings healing" (Prov. 12:18).

Randy's tongue was scarred from all the times he bit it! Instead of returning his boss's angry rhetoric, Randy would wait until his emotion was under control, then rationally discuss his feelings with his boss. Communicating our feelings when we are angry or when we are the subject of someone's anger is important. It is equally important that we communicate rationally instead of emotionally. Emotional, anger-charged communication can escalate a bad situation while rational, cooler communication can bring resolution and healing.

STEWARDSHIP

Imagine you are responsible for your friends' home while they are out of town. You are the steward of that home. You are to get the newspaper from the driveway each day and turn on different lights in the house to give the appearance that the residents are home. Suppose you let the newspapers pile up on the driveway and never change the lights. The home becomes an easy target for a thief.

We are stewards of our relationships. If we fail to express value, learn from our mistakes, and live a balanced life, then our relationships, like our friend's home, become an easy target for the thief called anger. We let our emotion pile up like newspapers on the driveway when we fail to communicate rationally our feelings, and an angry outburst is inevitable.

Stewardship means we take responsibility for our emotions and use them in a way that builds the object of our purpose—relationships.

ANGER AND YOUR CHARACTER EQUATION

1. What was the cause of your last bout with anger? Be specific.

2. In what ways was your significance threatened?
3. Does your response to question 2 suggest you need to clarify your life's purpose? If yes, look back to the chapters relating to purpose.
4. How could your practice of expressed value, learning, balance, accountability, communication, and stewardship be improved to help prevent or manage your anger more effectively in the future?

SIXTEEN

Mistakes and Failures

*J*eff and John's father owned a restaurant. The brothers grew up making daily visits to the eatery along with many people in their community. The restaurant was highly regarded. As the boys grew older, each was given a job in the restaurant.

John, the older of the pair, loved the business; and when he graduated from college, John returned home to help his father. Jeff never expressed much interest in the restaurant. In fact, Jeff moved to New York City when he graduated from college. Since Jeff was not interested in the restaurant, his dad eventually sold it to John.

John had big plans. He hired a first-class chef and added entrées and desserts to the menu. Later John renovated the building, making it possible to accommodate large groups. The changes were received well by his customers, and the business grew.

Meanwhile, Jeff was struggling in New York. He bounced from job to job, eventually waiting tables at a mediocre restaurant in Queens. The cost of living in New York more than consumed his earnings, leading Jeff to conclude he could wait tables at home in the family's restaurant. He called John, who enthusiastically invited Jeff to come home.

Jeff took the highly visible position of maître d'. In time the regular customers recognized Jeff as easily as John. The business continued to grow. Life was good until the day John arrived at the restaurant and found a note from Jeff saying, "Brother, Maurice (the chef) and I are opening our own restaurant." John felt as if he had been slugged in the gut! His own brother taking his prize chef and opening a competing business. Jeff had allowed his ambition to cloud his judgment.

John pressed forward, hiring a new chef and updating his menu. For a while, John's business declined. Many of his regular customers dined with

Jeff. After a few months, John began seeing his old customers come back. Soon John's business was even larger than before Jeff's departure.

One evening John was home when Jeff knocked on the door. Jeff came to tell John that his restaurant had flopped. Immediately John invited Jeff to come back to the "family" business. Was Jeff's departure a mistake or a failure?

We all make mistakes, but do we all fail? Remember these characters?

Clarence's cocaine habit was ultimately uncovered. He was caught, and he knew it the minute we sent him for a drug test. Was Clarence's drug habit a mistake or a failure?

Remember Mike, the clerk responsible for the redundant multimillion-dollar system error? He was not sure if his work was correct, but he did not ask anyone for help. Was Mike's decision not to seek help a mistake or a failure?

Was it a mistake or a failure when Leah's coworkers came to see me? These were the women upset because we had given Leah an extra break in the afternoon because of her difficult pregnancy.

What about these common situations most of us have faced:

- An addition error in your checkbook leads to an overdrawn account. Checks bounce, and fees pile up. Mistake or failure?
- You are so busy talking to someone in the car that you run a red light. The policeman is nice but writes the ticket, and your insurance rates go up. Mistake or failure?
- A friend at work tells you that a friend told her that yet another friend said you are fat. A few days later you run into the friend alleged to have made the unbecoming remark, and you quip, "You're not so thin yourself," only to find out this friend never made the offensive statement. Was your response a mistake or a failure?

Is it a mistake or a failure when we miss our sales goal? What about when we disappoint the people we love? Perhaps you regret a past decision or action. Is the regret the result of a mistake or a failure?

The answer to all of these situations is the same. These are mistakes, and we choose to allow these mistakes to become failures when we are unwilling to learn. Jeff made a mistake when he stiffed his brother. His mistake could have turned to failure had he not come back to John. Clarence made a mistake when he used cocaine. His mistake could have become a failure had he not stopped using. Mike's mistake was potentially expensive, but he learned, and we moved ahead. Leah's coworkers realized their pettiness and turned their mistake into positive action.

There is only one failure—the unwillingness to learn. The character equation solves the problem of failure by relating our practice to our purpose. Living by the character equation makes life a process, a series of mistakes that serve as learning experiences leading to a greater understanding of purpose. Apply the character equation.

THE CHARACTER EQUATION

PURPOSE

Have you wondered why our life's path is not clearly laid before us so each step toward the most meaningful purpose becomes obvious? Life is frustrating at times when you are attempting to clarify and move toward your purpose. The next step is not always clearly marked. In fact, the next step is rarely marked; and, as a result, we misstep from time to time.

For several reasons our missteps—our mistakes—are part of the process of understanding our purpose. First, we gain wisdom through the trials and errors of life. In theory we can avoid mistakes if we know the correct next step to take in any situation. Other than trial and error, divine intervention is the only way we could know the correct next step in any given situation. If God had intended to intervene in our lives, rendering us perfect, then Jeff would not have stiffed his brother, Clarence would not have snorted his paycheck, and Leah's coworkers would have given her their break instead of trying to take hers away.

Divine perfection is not possible for you and me in this life, which brings us back to trial and error. How do you know broccoli tastes bad? Because you have tried it, and the next time it is offered you know you don't want to eat it. How do you know Interstate 65 does not lead to Atlanta? Because you tried it and ended up in Birmingham. On your next trip to Atlanta, you will travel Interstate 85 because you recognize Interstate 65 is the wrong road.

Mistakes can become our teacher, leading us to a greater understanding of our purpose. How do you know a promising opportunity will not lead you toward your purpose? Probably because you have tried a similar road before and ended up in a place you hope never to visit again. Mistakes make us wiser if we are attentive to their teaching.

Mistakes confirm our purpose, and that is a second reason mistakes are part of the process of understanding purpose. Sometimes when a child errs, he receives a swift spanking. The mistake is punctuated with pain. The same lesson applies to adults in search of the meaning and stability only our purpose can offer. Mistakes create a clear contrast between the joy of purposeful living and the pain of Purpose Deficiency Syndrome. The pain of our mistakes causes us to long for the joy of our purpose.

The third reason mistakes are part of the purpose process is because mistakes become the currency for owning your purpose. We come to know the value of our purpose through the mistakes we make. It is a paradox, but the more we make mistakes and recover from them, the more we value our purpose. Recovering from a mistake means we learn and move ahead. Learning has not occurred if mistakes are recurring, that is, the same mistake is made over and over. In this paradox, mistakes indicate a progression toward purpose. Mistakes become the price we pay for understanding and living our purpose. Paying a price for our purpose naturally causes us to take ownership of seeing it become a reality.

Life should be considered as a journey and evaluated in its entirety. Taking the "long view," we can make mistakes and move ahead—knowing each step is making us wiser, confirming our purpose, and helping us take ownership of its accomplishment.

EXPRESSED VALUE

Mistakes bring with them unparalleled opportunities to express value to those in your work world. Clarence was hopeless because he believed his addiction was a permanent part of his life. Making matters worse, Clarence did not see a reason to live. The addiction blocked any vision Clarence may have had regarding his purpose. Devoid of purpose, Clarence placed little if any value on himself. He lost his will to live.

Expressing value places importance on the person rather than the performance. Clarence grew up in a home where performance was the way to earn his parents' affection. Now his consistently poor performance and his addiction, left Clarence feeling of little intrinsic worth. We expressed how much we valued Clarence by intervening in his addiction and getting help for him. Our message was that you are of great value, a person with tremendous purpose. In time and with regular contact, Clarence began to see the possibilities of his life.

ENCOURAGEMENT

Mistakes at work can create instability and insecurity. Mike made a potentially multimillion-dollar mistake. He feared that his mistake might result in his termination of employment. In many cases such a mistake would justify termination, but in Mike's case I felt he was due another opportunity. I knew Mike could handle the job with proper training, but the experience caused Mike to question his own ability. Before we could move ahead, Mike had to believe he was capable of handling the job. Encouraging Mike to improved performance was my job. I encouraged Mike by working directly with him periodically to improve his skill and knowledge. In this instance I encouraged Mike with hands-on training. As a result, Mike gained the confidence to perform his duties with excellence.

Encouragement balances expressed value by communicating that the person is capable of performing the task at hand. Expressed value focuses on the innate worth of the person. Encouragement builds on that foundation by focusing the person on the task.

LEARNING

Builders take a pile of brick and, one by one, set them in place as they construct a home. We are building our lives every second of every day. Mistakes are inevitable, and they can be helpful in fulfilling our purpose. Mistakes are like the bricks. When we make a mistake, we can choose to ignore it by throwing it into a pile out of view, or we can learn from it by methodically and intentionally putting the mistake in its proper place.

The critical difference between mistakes and failure is learning. Jeff went too long ignoring his mistakes. He was on the brink of a failure, an unwillingness to learn, when he turned to his brother. The character equation is constructed to keep you focused on those actions that will lead you back to your purpose.

BALANCE

Understanding your mistakes in the context of the entirety of your life requires a healthy perspective. How many of us really have this perspective? Every advertiser on television hopes to shape your perspective. Every preacher in every pulpit hopes to shape your perspective. Most movie producers hope to shape your perspective. Indeed, I hope to shape your perspective through this book.

The evidence is overwhelming that those intent on shaping and changing our perspectives are succeeding. Personal debt is at an all-time high. The number of hours worked each week is growing to record levels. Americans are increasingly obese. Roughly 50 percent of all marriages end in divorce. We are under unusual stress, and with these confused perspectives we are trying to make sense of our lives, especially the mistakes we make.

Leah was difficult to work with before she was pregnant. Leah's perspective about her infertility was harshly out of balance. The result of her imbalanced perspective was to ignore the obvious relationship problems that plagued her work. Leah let those mistakes pile up like bricks on a job site. Before she knew it, the pile of mistakes was bigger than she was capable of handling. Leah's pregnancy saved her work relationships because her perspective was vastly different. Once pregnant, Leah became more objective, and she confronted the pile of mistakes she had ignored for so long. One by one she worked her way through her mistakes, taking notes about each one. Leah wanted to learn, and she did.

ACCOUNTABILITY

Mike thought he had covered up his mistakes. Clarence thought no one knew he was using cocaine again. Can you recall a recent mistake you have made? If not, I am certain a coworker can help jog your memory.

We need help jogging our memories from time to time. More importantly, we need help preventing mistakes. Accountability is that help. Knowing you are going to give an account for your work at a regular meeting is a compelling tool that reminds you to keep a healthy perspective and to minimize mistakes. Who is your accountability partner?

MISTAKES AND FAILURES AND THE CHARACTER EQUATION

1. Record the events surrounding a recent mistake you have made.
2. How did others respond to your mistake? How did you respond to your mistake?
3. How could you have handled that issue better?
4. What did you learn from that experience? What have you learned from this exercise of rethinking the mistake?

SEVENTEEN

Victory, Success, and Significance

*A*merica is obsessed with achievement and recognition, and we equate each with success. Look around. Fortune 500 lists the biggest, most successful companies. *Forbes* publishes its list of Americans who have accumulated the most financial wealth. *INC.* publishes its list of the 100 most successful small companies. We recognize the entrepreneur of the year, man or woman of the year, athlete of the year, and on and on. In sports the polls rank our alma maters based on their record of wins. We crown the national champion and even presumptuously the world champion (what about the Japanese teams) in major league baseball. Our children spend most of a week in school taking achievement tests, and we rank our schools according to the results.

I am a competitive person and believe competition is healthy when kept in perspective. When we break the rules—and indeed the law—in order to achieve greater results, we have lost that healthy perspective. Consider the number of Wall Street firms fined and the number of their employees barred from the securities industry because they broke the law during the "junk bond" era. When alumni break the NCAA rules and pay student athletes to play at their schools, we have lost that healthy perspective. The list of universities cited for infractions is long and includes everyone from UCLA to Slippery Rock to Kansas State to Grambling. The loss of perspective can be seen even at the high school and junior high school levels. I played for the Cloverdale Junior High School basketball team. Our ninth-grade year we were defeated by three points in the state championship game but were later awarded the top prize when it was learned our opponent had played three of its senior high school players in the junior high tournament against us.

135

Why do we pay college players? Why do high school coaches cheat in an effort to win? Why do daddies get into fistfights at Little League parks? The answer is linked to our obsession with achievement and recognition. According to Mary Bell, founder and executive director of the Center for Recovering Families, "Achievement is the alcohol of our time. These days, the best people don't abuse alcohol. They abuse their lives."[1] Bell is pointing out that many people break the rules physically and morally in an effort to achieve and gain recognition and this obsession ultimately brings the person down.

Achievement is good, but like all good things taken to an extreme, achievement can become our weakness. Our orientation toward achievement has produced the largest number of millionaires in history—more than 3.5 million people. For the first time in history, more millionaires are under the age of fifty than above it. Such achievement, such success has never before been seen, but at the same time more and more people are being diagnosed with depression. More than seventeen million people in the United States suffer from some form of depression. Some twenty-two million people take the mood-altering drugs Zoloft and Prozac.[2] If we are achieving such unprecedented success, why are we growing ever more depressed?

Francis Ford Coppola is regarded as one of the most successful directors in Hollywood. His films include *Apocalypse Now, Patton, The Rainmaker,* and *The Godfather. The Godfather* is one of the most financially successful movies in history, so you would expect Coppola to count this movie among his greatest successes, right? Here is Coppola's view of this successful movie: "People are shocked to hear that I think of *The Godfather* series with sadness. I see those films almost as a personal failure. They changed my life dramatically, even though the world treated them as big artistic and commercial successes. Their success led me to make big commercial films—when what I really wanted was to do original films, like those Woody Allen is able to focus on."[3]

Coppola may have provided an answer to the paradox of increasing emotional distress in the midst of unprecedented success. Coppola considered *The Godfather* "almost as a personal failure" because he allowed the achievement and resulting recognition to lead him in a direction he did not wish to go. Coppola felt his purpose was more directed to original films, but he followed the path to big commercial films. His practice did not match his purpose. Coppola had a case of Purpose Deficiency Syndrome.

No one argued with Coppola's decision to produce blockbuster movies. After all, he had succeeded in producing a grand scale movie in *The*

Godfather; and such a commercial success, such an achievement, is the goal, right? Coppola's dilemma is not unique to him. Workplaces are full of people whose practice does not match their purpose, and they are experiencing a lack of fulfillment and meaning. Maybe we have pursued goals that conventional wisdom says bring success only to find them hollow and meaningless.

Life is a quest for fulfillment, stability, and meaning. Our world treats success as the key to finding fulfillment, stability, and success. Coppola and others who have experienced success might disagree. Perhaps success is not enough to satisfy our soul's longing for fulfillment, stability, and meaning. Coppola is enormously successful; but because his practice did not lead to his purpose, he viewed his achievement as "almost a personal failure." Coppola made his judgment about his success and failure looking back over the achievements of his life in relation to his purpose. He measured his success or failure against the test of time and his purpose. Time and purpose are the missing pieces in the definition of success. Perhaps a new definition of *success* is needed.

The traditional definition of *success* is, "The achievement of something attempted." This definition of *success* can deliver fulfillment, stability, and meaning because it ignores their prerequisite—purpose. Was the success purposeful? Did the success move you toward your purpose? If not, Coppola might tell us the achievement was not at all successful.

I define *victory* as "the achievement of something attempted." Victory is winning the everyday battles we face. We can win the battle and lose the war of living a successful life. That is the difference between victory and success.

Success and victory are different. Success includes the element of purpose. My definition of *success* reads, "The achievement of purposeful milestones." Success is winning the purposeful battle. Success requires that we attempt projects and achieve milestones that move us toward our purpose. Milestones are achievements along a journey, steps along the way. Success is purposeful achievement, and it leads us to our ultimate goal—significance.

Significance is our goal, and it is measured only once, when we come to the end of our lives. Significance yields fulfillment, stability, and meaning. Our definition of *significance* reads, "The fulfillment of our purpose measured at the end of our lives." Significance is the result of our successes leading us to the fulfillment of our purpose over our lifetime.

We tend to allow our culture to declare someone a success before the all-important tally at the end of life. Mickey Mantle was certainly touted as a huge success, but his life ended miserably after years of alcohol abuse.

137

Marilyn Monroe continues to be among the most famous actresses to have lived, but all that fame and fortune did not stop her from committing suicide. These people claimed success when they should have declared victory. Victory is setting the batting record. Success is consistently setting the record over your career and understanding how that victory fulfilled your purpose. Victory is landing the star role in the movie. Success is consistently landing the star role and understanding how that victory fulfilled your purpose.

Victories can be stepping-stones toward success.

Our victories should help us discern which milestones to attempt. *The Godfather* was a victory for Coppola; and looking back, he learned such a movie was not successful because it was not consistent with his purpose. Coppola may achieve his purpose and significance by attempting purposeful milestones in the future. Victories are fine as long as they lead us to understand what will make us successful in the future.

Recall James Dobson's statement, "When you come to the end of your life, the only thing that will matter is who you loved, who loved you, and what you did for your Creator." The character equation keeps us focused on the purpose and practice of life, so when we come to the end of our lives, we will have succeeded in the things that matter and will have achieved significance.

PURPOSE

Success is defined by our purpose. Coppola, Mantle, and Monroe allowed society to define success for them. When the world declares a person successful, there can be a sense of finality, a feeling that "I have done it; I have arrived." Once a person entertains those thoughts, the urgency to practice a purposeful life can become less important. That is when Purpose Deficiency Syndrome takes root, and we lose our way. Life becomes unfulfilling, and we live with regret.

Coppola listened to the critics and allowed their praise to replace his purpose. He looked back with a measure of regret. Mantle allowed the cheering crowds and his victorious records to replace his purpose. He fed his lack of fulfillment with booze, and his life ended without significance. The enormously popular Marilyn Monroe took her own life when she could no longer reconcile her purpose and practice. Though she continues to be highly regarded, Marilyn's life cannot be considered significant. These people enjoyed victories, but their victories did not lead them to success or significance.

Distinguishing victory and success begins with the process of developing your purpose statement. Your purpose statement focuses your abilities, passions, and relationships toward the fulfillment of your life's best possible result. Your purpose is your life's best possible result, and successes are the good things that occur along the journey. Sometimes we allow that which is good (victories) to oppose that which is best (purpose). Coppola, Mantle, and Monroe are great examples. How can we keep our focus on our purpose? Here are a few ideas:

- Review your purpose statement and ask yourself, "Is this statement about my daily victories or my life's purpose?" Your statement is about victories if achievement of specific goals, such as a sales goal, is addressed rather than how hitting that goal will afford you the opportunity to impact others. If your statement is about victories, begin work on it again. Chapters 1–3 will be helpful.
- List the successes necessary each day, month, and year to move you toward your purpose. Plan to celebrate your successes, acknowledging them as a step in the process of living a life that, if you continue on the path, will be judged significant.
- Be prepared to correct a well-intended friend when he or she applauds your significance. Tell the friend you have won a purposeful battle but the jury is still out regarding your significance.
- Become thankful for your purpose—whatever it is. Our society recognizes some accomplishments and ignores others. Human nature desires recognition, but our world may never recognize the successes leading to the significance. Ironically, Marilyn Monroe gained great recognition from others, but that recognition was less powerful than her need to be fulfilled. Know your purpose and personally acknowledge its significance.

EXPRESSED VALUE

You are a person of intrinsic and infinite worth. The only way to enhance your worth is by fulfilling your purpose. But what about Bill Gates? His victories have brought him billions. Remember that significance is judged when we look back over our life. On that day Bill Gates will leave his billions behind. The only thing that will matter to Gates on that day is the fulfillment of his purpose.

Relationships are the object of our purpose, and expressed value is the measure of how we have applied our purpose. Successes bring the opportunity to express value toward others. Certainly you would congratulate someone when he or she achieves a success, but in that moment you have a prime opportunity to acknowledge their intrinsic worth. For example, a friend of Mickey Mantle's might say (if it is true), "That was a tremendous home run, but I want you to know that as great a hit as it was, you are a better friend than home-run hitter."

We need to express value to others and ourselves in the euphoria of a momentary success, to be reminded that we are purposed for even greater success. We need to express value to keep our perspective on the fulfillment of our purpose so we will be judged significant.

BALANCE

Balance requires that we define the dimensions of our lives and organize them around our purpose. All of our dimensions—intellectual, physical, spiritual, and social—must be emphasized and nurtured if we hope to achieve a balanced life. Emphasizing and nurturing our dimensions also helps keep success in perspective.

Many people emphasize the intellectual dimension through our work at the expense of the other three. We become workaholics, and our perspective narrows to this one dimension. When we eat, sleep, and breathe in one dimension, we naturally see the potential for success there and there only. Our obsession with achievement and recognition pushes us deeper and deeper into this one dimension because it has become the only area where we can experience success. Now one dimensional in our perspective, our mistakes can devastate us, and our successes can cause us to think we have achieved true significance.

Maintaining balance in our lives brings the perspective we need to understand that our successes can be steps in the direction of significance but not the achievement of significance. The balanced person can be successful in his work, but the euphoria of the success is tempered by his knowledge of weak points in other areas of his life. The ongoing process of maintaining balance is humbling because there will always be a dimension in need of growth and attention. Mickey Mantle may have been so caught up in the victories of his work that he felt invincible. That "king of the world" feeling led Mantle to abuse his body with alcohol.

Mickey needed balance. We all need balance to take our victories in stride. Balance helps you understand that your victories can be one step toward success leading to significance, the fulfillment of your purpose measured at the end of your life. You can take a step toward balance by saying no to activities that do not lead you to your purpose. You move toward balance when you are victorious and consistently ask, "That was a great victory in my work, but was it aligned with my purpose? In what area of my life am I falling down on the job?"

ACCOUNTABILITY

My grandmother, Thelma Williams, was a wise woman. She seemed always to have the right words for any situation. One of her quips of wisdom provided me a measure of accountability in the midst of a victory. If I had been victorious in some endeavor to the point of believing I was invincible, she would bring me back to reality by saying, "Just remember, you put your britches on the same way the other guys do." That is accountability!

In 1956, Mickey Mantle won the Triple Crown—a .353 batting average, 52 home runs, and 130 runs batted in. I can imagine how Mantle might have felt invincible, like he had arrived at the point of success. Mantle would have benefited from some straight talk from my grandmother, reminding him that he put his "britches on the same way the other guys do."

In the summer of 1995, Mickey Mantle looked back and judged his life to be unsuccessful. Mantle met the press, his body riddled with cancer and dying, and declared, "Don't be like me, I'm no role model!"[4] Accountability early in his life may have led Mickey away from his destructive behavior and toward a balanced life. Perhaps accountability would have compelled Mantle to use his victories as stepping-stones to success leading to significance. Accountability may make the same difference in your life.

Family and close friends are the best accountability partners because they know we "put our britches on like everyone else." Others think we are special because of our momentary victories. Family and close friends know we are special because of our life's purpose, and their close proximity to us allows them to see our weaknesses. Family and close friends celebrate our momentary victories, but they remind us of our purpose and our weaknesses. They help keep our feet on the ground. Family and close friends help us grow toward our purpose. Have you empowered a family member or close friend to hold you accountable to grow toward your purpose?

SERVICE

Custom One Homes is a fast-growing home builder in Atlanta. Owner Steve Tucker started his company "to serve the needs" of both his customer and employee. There is a difference between "to serve the needs" and "providing service."

"To serve the needs" is a focus on the other person for the benefit of the other person. This mind-set is constantly checking motives by asking the why questions. Why and for whose benefit are we growing? The "to serve the needs" perspective views service as its platform for accomplishing its purpose.

"Providing service" is a focus on the other person for "my" benefit. The question here is, How much can we grow and how quickly? The "providing service" mind-set views its service as a way to make a living.

Steve Tucker's business exists "to serve the needs" of others. He plans, monitors, and controls the growth of his company to ensure Custom One Homes is serving the needs of others, not just his own. Tucker formed a foundation, and every year a percentage of Custom One Homes' profit is contributed—based on Custom One employees' joint decision—to other groups who are in the business "to serve the needs." Keeping the "to serve the needs" perspective is a daily battle, so Tucker loaded up the personnel of the whole company and took them to Mexico, where they spent a week building houses for the homeless.

Service is meeting others' needs for their benefit. A met need is a success, a stepping-stone to the fulfillment of our purpose. Adopting the "to serve the needs" perspective opens our eyes to the vast depth of need that exists and our limited ability to meet those needs. This mind-set will not allow us to be satisfied meeting a need here and a need there or to provide service for selfish gain. Instead, the success of a met need compels us to meet the next need and the next and the next. What about your service? For whose benefit are you meeting needs?

INTEGRITY

Mickey Mantle looked back in his last days with regret. Francis Ford Coppola added up his life to date "as almost a personal failure." Both Mantle and Coppola realized they had missed their purpose, and with respect to character and purpose these two high achievers blew their integrity. Integrity is consistently practicing a purposeful life.

Our victories and successes are a test of integrity. Coppola's victory, *The Godfather* series, opened many doors; and he chose the door that led to big commercial films. Integrity to his purpose would have led him to walk through the door leading to smaller original films. Mantle's victories afforded him a place in the Baseball Hall of Fame. Integrity to his purpose would have afforded him an even greater place as a role model for young men and women.

In the midst of victory, we are challenged not to trade our integrity for what the world calls success. Seeking achievement and recognition does not bring true success or significance. True success and significance depend on our integrity—consistently practicing a purposeful life.

VICTORY, SUCCESS, SIGNIFICANCE, AND THE CHARACTER EQUATION

Well-known but quirky defense attorney Gerry Spence observes, "We view success in this country as the accumulation of money. If you have money, you're beautiful. If you have money, you're wise. If you have money, you're good. If you have money, you're successful. Money stands for every single virtue there is, and what we should do is change the definition of *success* so that success depends on personhood. You're successful because you're a true person."[5] I do not always agree with Gerry Spence, but in this instance he is absolutely right. Perhaps Spence will accept this definition of *success*, "the achievement of purposeful milestones," and this definition of *significance*, "the fulfillment of our purpose measured at the end of our lives."

1. How is your desire for achievement and recognition out of balance?
2. List ten of your personal victories from the past twelve months. Then describe how each victory is either leading you toward or away from your purpose.
3. How are you keeping your victories and successes in perspective? Do you have an accountability partner?
4. Are you working "to serve the needs" of others or "to provide service"?

EIGHTEEN

Ethics and Decision Making

he well-known economist Milton Friedman once said, "The only obligation of a business is to make a profit."[1] Do you agree with Friedman? The implications of Friedman's comment are far-reaching.

First, Friedman's comment nixes the need for enlightenment of any corporate purpose other than the purpose of producing a profit. This makes simple the whole question of purpose; but this simplicity comes at the expense of shareholders, customers, and even employees. A single-minded focus on profit may give incentive to maximizing current earnings at the expense of investments that would pay off for the shareholder in the future. Customers may find their purchase to be made of increasingly lower quality materials, thereby enhancing the earnings of its maker. Employees may find their benefits eroding year after year even as their employer's earnings rise.

The single-minded pursuit of profit can have devastating effects on a company's shareholders, but in Friedman's "profit only" world, this is OK because a company follows profit wherever it is and by whatever means it takes to get it. Expediency, compromised quality, and broken promises are tools of the "profit only" trade. Practitioners of this mind-set take little if any responsibility for the manner profit is derived. In their world, profit itself determines the way business is conducted.

Friedman would certainly argue the "profit only" perspective is not illegal, at least it is not intentionally illegal. It is true that trading long-term profit for short-term profit is not illegal. It is true that compromised quality is not illegal, and it is true that continually devaluing employee benefits is not necessarily illegal. The law, however, is the absolute minimum standard of practice for any business, organization, or individual. It goes without saying that any legitimate business, organization, or individual—including the "profit only" crowd—sets out to operate legally. But problems arise in the pursuit of profit when one competitor lowers the standard of practice. Without external, objective standards of practice, the practitioner's only option is to meet his competitor in the filth of ever-lowering standards. Sometimes these standards violate the law.

Jeb Stuart Magruder, one of the Watergate conspirators, commenting on the Watergate scandal, wrote, "We had conned ourselves into thinking we weren't doing anything really wrong, and by the time we were doing things that were illegal, we had lost control. We had gone from poor ethical behavior into illegal activities without even realizing it." A problem with Friedman's "profit only" mind-set is that good men and women like Magruder and others rationalize their unethical behavior as the necessary means to obtain the profit and even if that behavior does not prove to be illegal it almost always is devastating to someone in their path.

I have heard a myth throughout my career that says, "To succeed in business you must do business the way business demands." In other words, profit is the objective, so get it any way you can. This myth is Friedman's "profit only" practice, and many people have bought the myth. Consider the following cases:

> After being notified that eight airplanes his company worked on had been grounded—a situation for which his company's parts could be responsible—the CEO had to decide how much to disclose to his bankers, his employees, his investors, and his auditors. Although he weighed many factors in deciding whom and how much to tell, the CEO admitted that he never once considered the lives that could be at stake. That, he felt, was the Federal Aviation Administration's burden. "What do I know about engines?" the CEO reasoned, by way of defending his oversight. "As a businessman, I was looking at this in terms of my survival."[2]

> Archer Daniels Midland Co.—self-described "Supermarket to the World"—and three of its former executives have been found to have engaged in a massive global conspiracy to fix the price of lysine, a heretofore obscure livestock feed additive.[3]

The list of ethical breaches is long. When an individual, company, or organization bites the dust of unethical behavior, their actions affect the future decisions of those watching. Those watching can choose to follow the poor example of the unethical, or they can choose to learn from the bad behavior and raise the standard. Fortunately, many corporations and individuals have addressed the issue of ethical decision making.

Some companies have implemented ethics programs, and some have hired an ethics director. Companies with a formal ethics program often enjoy better financial performance than those companies without a formal ethics program. "Those companies that use progressive grievance procedures, incentive programs, information sharing, and job designs have much better financial performance than those without, according to a Rutgers University survey."[4] The problem with this statistic is that it could lead a CEO to implement an ethics program for the wrong reasons. A CEO, indeed a "profit only" CEO, could choose to implement an ethics program to boost profits. But what if profits do not rise? What if the new ethics department does not generate the expected profits? Chop, Chop! No more ethics department. Ethics programs are great, but such a program should be implemented because of conscience and not profitability.

Friedman's "profit only" approach appeals to our most basic adversary—selfishness. We are constantly at war with our selfish nature, and losing the battle leaves us vulnerable to ethical compromise.

How do you know what decision to make in a given circumstance? When asked to handle a situation in a way that your conscience questions, how do you discern the ethical response? The next time you are concerned about a decision, ask these questions:

1. Does this decision support my purpose?
   - Will this decision build my relationships or damage my relationships?
   - Does this decision use or build my abilities?
   - Am I passionate about this decision?
2. Does this decision support my company's purpose?
3. Can I carry out this decision in a manner consistent with my desired practice of life?
4. How will the report of this decision look in the newspaper?

The character equation can be used as an ethics test.

THE CHARACTER EQUATION

PURPOSE

When facing a question with an unclear answer, you might ask, "Does this decision support my purpose?" Individual and corporate purpose always raises the standard of acceptable practice. True purpose depends on an ethical practice for its fulfillment. You can be assured of staying on the ethical path if your decision supports your purpose.

Friedman limits purpose to the mere achievement of profit. His is a purpose of serving yourself, and such a purpose breeds expediency. Solomon wrote, "Where there is no revelation, the people cast off restraint" (Prov. 29:18). A purpose that does not include the building of relationships and the development of our abilities and passions is no purpose at all. When we operate under the illusion of the "profit only" mind-set, we are managing without a proper understanding of purpose; and in the heat of the battle we turn and go our own way. The CEO of the airplane repair company was the personification of the "profit only" mind-set. His only purpose was the self-gratification and self-indulgence of profit. In the midst of a crisis, the CEO went his own way and passed the buck to the FAA. The CEO's purpose in life amounted to nothing, so it is understandable why his practice of life was so poor.

EXPRESSED VALUE

Climbing the corporate ladder can be tough. Workloads are handed out and increased in a effort to see who is serious about their work. The serious put in extra hours to get the job done, and they progress to the next rung. Sometimes, however, requests are made that are ethically questionable. Your boss gives you a $1,000 bonus and simultaneously directs you to give a $1,000 contribution to a certain political campaign. Your boss is constantly inviting you to eat lunch with him and his secretary. A month and 15 lunches later you discover the boss and his secretary are having an affair, and you have unwittingly been made an accomplice because your presence allowed the pair to spend time together without the liaison appearing to be one on one. The price-fixing conspirators at ADM, the World's Supermarket, probably involved a number of lower-level executives in the scheme.

If asked to compromise your ethics, then you can be sure you are not valued by the person making the request. If you were highly valued by your boss, why would he put you in a compromising position? We express value to others when we call them to raise the standard. We express value to others when we witness an ethical breach and help them change. We express value to ourselves when we link up with an employer or employee whose purposeful life has produced a visible ethical practice.

If you are asked to do something that is unethical, you have two choices: You can change your team of people, or you can get off the team. In other words, if unethical actions are a regular occurrence, you can work to improve the ethics of those around you; and if that has been attempted and proven not to be possible, then you can move on to another employer.

LEARNING

Perhaps you have compromised your ethics. Maybe you are the guy having lunch with your boss and his secretary, or your boss at ADM let you in on the price-fixing scheme. Now what do you do?

First, you must acknowledge your ethical breach. Look yourself in the mirror and describe your actions out loud so you can hear your own words. You must take responsibility for what you have done. Next, forgive yourself. Verbalize your forgiveness out loud so you can again hear your own words. Ask the affected parties to forgive you. Such an uncommon act will start the healing process for you and others. Finally, make restitution. If possible and if warranted, repay the injured party.

Like Magruder, you may wake up to your own rationalizations only to find you too have crossed the ethical line if not the legal line. The ethical breach can be compounded if you continue to rationalize your actions. Your actions can be redeemed if you learn from the ethical lapse and move ahead and allow others to do the same. Learning is the redemptive process necessary for cleaning up the mess of unethical behavior.

ACCOUNTABILITY

Accountability is the insurance we need to prohibit the breach of ethics. Accountability may have saved ADM the embarrassment of the price-fixing scandal. Magruder and the White House crew could have changed history with just a little accountability.

CEOs tell me frequently that they have no accountability. Most CEOs have boards of directors, but let's face the facts: Boards of directors often rubber-stamp management's decisions. Most boards offer little accountability until there is a problem. We work with CEOs in the capacity of an executive coach.[5] In this role we regularly discuss the issues the CEO and his/her company is facing, holding them accountable to their purpose and stated practice.

Anyone, regardless of position on the corporate ladder, who models ethical behavior is a powerful teacher. We work with CEOs in this capacity because the CEO is one of the best teachers of ethical or unethical practices. The CEO teaches as he/she models these practices each day.

Accountability is not just for CEOs although CEOs certainly need accountability to maintain their personal integrity as well as accountability to lead the company toward its purpose. The rest of the crew—managers and the rank and file—need accountability to accept the authority of the employer, work in alignment with the company's purpose, and maintain personal integrity.

We all need accountability because the lure of the "profit only" mind-set is strong, even appealing. Our purpose stands as an objective accountability partner. When faced with an ethical dilemma, our stated purpose offers guidance.

SERVICE

George Marshall, owner of TriState Reprographics located in Pittsburgh, Pennsylvania, has built a reputation among his customers for understanding and meeting their needs. Customers phone in orders, and on some days the TriState representative recognizes the customer's request is not what the customer actually needs. TriState's practice is to spend time educating customers so they will better understand their needs and so customers can change their order to fit their true need.

The TriState approach is uncommon, and it is ethical. In most workplaces the company representative will simply take the order regardless of its relationship to the customer's actual need. In these instances the customer often spends more money than is necessary. The TriState approach sometimes results in less revenue. However, keeping your ethical edge in the customer relationship requires you to keep an unwavering focus on their needs.

INTEGRITY

Imagine becoming so obsessed with the achievement of a certain goal—presidential race, profitability race, or a self-preservation race—that you trade one of the few things you truly can control—your integrity. You never intended to trade away this most intimate, defining characteristic; but suddenly you have lost it, and the only person responsible for its loss is you.

The Airplane Repair Company may have survived, but the CEO lost his integrity. ADM still claims to be the world's supermarket; but the ADM management team is out of work, having lost that which is more important than feeding the world—personal integrity.

ETHICS, DECISION MAKING, AND THE CHARACTER EQUATION

1. In what ways have you practiced the "profit only" mind-set?
2. What changes do you need to make to become more aligned with your purpose?
3. Think of an instance when someone asked you to do something unethical? How did that make you feel?
4. What system of accountability do you have in place today that will help ensure your continued ethical behavior?

NINETEEN

Hiring and Firing

ait! This chapter is for you even if you are not in management. "But I don't have responsibility for hiring and firing," you say; but you are wrong. Managers hire and sometimes fire employees. Everyone hires and sometimes fires their employer. When you chose to work for a company or organization, you are in effect making the same choice your new boss made in hiring you. You are hiring your employer. The principles of hiring and firing are as valid for the prospective employee interviewing a prospective employer as they are valid for the employer interviewing the prospective employee.

Tom, a stockbroker, called me to discuss a potential job change. He had received unsolicited calls from two firms just three days apart. Both firms were attractive to Tom for different reasons. Firm A, a New York Stock Exchange member brokerage firm, offered him a sizable signing bonus and the potential of becoming the branch manager in a few years. Several highly successful brokers in that office would be retiring in a few years, and Tom would be in position to assume their accounts.

Firm B was a financial planning firm. Their offer was a guaranteed salary plus a year-end bonus based on the amount of money his office managed. At the time of their offer, the firm's office employed five people who were tremendous analysts but rather lackluster salesmen. The firm wanted Tom to partner with the analysts as the salesperson for the office.

The offers came at a time when Tom was breaking all the sales records of his employer. He was happily employed and had not even thought about making a change until the other firms made their offers. Tom was confused and asked me, "What should I do?"

It is a small world. In the weeks before the firms called Tom, they called me! Firm A called and inquired: "Bill, we are looking for a person to work in our office there. We need someone who is management material but can also sell. Do you know anyone?" I bumped into the president of Firm B while on business in Grand Rapids, Michigan, and he asked me if I knew a stockbroker who would like to move into financial planning. These guys had an employment issue, and they were asking the same question as Tom, "What should I do?"

Questions often beg other questions, and such was the case with Tom and his prospective employers. The following questions relate to three principles of positive employment decisions. The answers to the questions below can be used in answering the ultimate employment question, What should I do?

1. Hire competency
Employer question: Does the prospective employee possess the abilities necessary to accomplish the task?
Employee question: Does the prospective position draw on my strengths or my weaknesses?

2. Hire compatibly
Employer question: Does the prospective employee exhibit a passion for the business?
Employee question: Am I passionate about this business?

3. Hire character
Employer question: Has the prospective employee demonstrated character in any of his/her experience?
Employee question: Based on a review of the prospective employer, what evidence exists that their practice is consistent with my desired practice?

People are changing jobs at an increasingly faster rate. We are regularly asking that important question, "What should I do?" Regarding an employment issue, this question is one of the most important questions you will ever ask. The hiring decision ultimately makes or breaks the manager. Hiring the right employer is also critical to the future of the employee. Yet we often approach it casually. Managers sometimes hire the first available candidate that breathes. Employees sometimes drift from company to company without giving thought to the long-term implications of their moves.

John owns and operates a lettuce-processing plant. His main business is selling lettuce to grocery store chains in twenty-four of the fifty states. For years John's loss ratio, the percentage of lettuce deemed unsuitable for delivery to their client and therefore trashed, concerned him. Fully 60 percent of John's lettuce harvest ended up in the trash bin due to size and/or color specifications. He had an idea of turning his waste into cash by selling it to restaurants and schools. John believed restaurants and schools would buy his unwanted lettuce because they are less likely to be concerned about the size or color, and his price would be quite cheap.

John is a no-nonsense, "get it done" guy. He makes a decision and takes action almost immediately. John decided to create a sales position to sell their unusable lettuce. He announced the opening in all the usual places—the newspaper, the break room bulletin board, and industry publications.

Within a week a local woman, Carol, responded to the announcement by making application. Carol was a computer salesperson of technical systems. She consistently exceeded her sales goal, and her employer was pleased with her performance. Carol, however, was not as pleased with her employer. In fact, Carol was tired of her boss's harsh tone and poor communication skills. Her boss often put Carol in the difficult position of selling a product before it had been tested. Carol was excited by the possibility of tackling a new job in a new industry. Plus, John's performance evaluation system inspired her confidence both in John and herself. The periodic evaluations would give Carol advance warning if she was getting off track.

John felt the interview with Carol went well. He spoke for almost one hour about the history of the company and where he thought the company was headed. John implied to Carol that this position was his highest priority and would be given the funding necessary to make it successful. John offered Carol the job at the end of the interview, and Carol promptly accepted.

Carol's first few months working for John were hectic. She immersed herself in learning everything about her product. After several months Carol knew the optimum soil for growing lettuce, the growing season, and every detail of processing the crop.

John developed a pattern of pulling Carol off her direct duties to help with other areas of the business. Such interruptions to her routine were frustrating; but while working with her coworkers, Carol learned a curious fact: her coworkers had no knowledge of her project. Carol was dumbfounded, given the emphasis John promised he would bring to her work.

Carol had been on the job about two months when John began making comments about her sales, specifically that she had not sold the first head of lettuce. Carol made volumes of calls each day to restaurant chains, restaurant distributors, and schools. She found the purchasing agents hard to persuade because their analysis of her offer only confirmed the practice of purchasing lettuce locally. Making her job more difficult, these potential customers were not concerned at all about the technical characteristics of Carol's product.

Carol confirmed John's initial belief that the restaurant and school markets were less concerned with size and color. Timely delivery and the total cost of the product were the decision points for purchasing agents. The cost of Carol's lettuce together with the shipping charge proved more expensive than the price the restaurants and schools paid at the local grocery store. It was evident John had not finished his homework before offering the job to Carol.

The obstacles Carol faced did not impress John, and he applied more and more pressure. Carol was struggling emotionally and physically. Some mornings Carol's work-induced nausea caused her to vomit. John's demeanor toward Carol had progressively changed from treating her like a superstar when she arrived to displaying frustration with her lack of production to intermittent bouts of screaming demeaning messages to ignoring her. Carol knew she was headed toward a firing, but was Carol going to fire John or was John going to fire Carol?

John fired Carol, and she was shocked even though she knew firing was the likely outcome of her employment. Carol expected John to give her some probationary period to turn things around, but instead he gave her about an hour to clean out her desk.

The employment decision is one of the most important decisions made for both the employee and the employer. The character equation is a standard that brings structure to the decision-making process. Consider how the following variables could have helped Carol and John make a better employment decision and at the very least end their employment without ending their relationship.

THE CHARACTER EQUATION

PURPOSE

John's idea appeared great, but he skipped the critical step of aligning his idea with the purpose of his business. For more than twenty-five years John's business had focused on grocery stores. John and his employees understood their business in the context of that market. Now John was appropriately beginning to broaden his customer base, which would change his company's purpose and therefore its culture.

John was responsible for preparing his company's culture for the change in purpose and establishing an environment giving Carol every possible advantage of achieving her goal. In his rush to turn the idea into action, John forgot to inform his employees. That explains why Carol's coworkers did not know what she was doing. Since these longtime employees continued to understand their company purpose in the context of serving grocery stores only, they placed little value on Carol's work. John had difficulty changing his paradigm from the traditional company purpose to the new broader purpose. That is why John constantly interrupted Carol's effort to have her complete projects unrelated to her function.

John was responsible for understanding the requirements of the job so he could assess the competency and the ability of potential candidates and choose the best fit for the position from among them. John's role is to select people whose abilities and passion, indeed purpose, are aligned with the company's purpose. Instead, John moved from good idea to announcing the position to hiring Carol, the first person interviewed.

The employment decision involves mutual responsibility. John had responsibility to offer the job to the most compatible candidate, but Carol shared that responsibility. Carol was a high achiever in her computer sales position because her technical skills added value for her customers. Carol was a detail person selling a detailed and unique product. She accepted a position selling a commodity, a common product where price and service are the only characteristics that distinguish it from the competition. Carol shouldered the responsibility for aligning her abilities and passions, her purpose, with the purpose of the position and the company.

Carol should have asked John more questions during the interview, and she should have asked herself more questions before the interview. Carol may have taken this job because she was frustrated and hurt with the manner in which her former boss communicated. Carol may have jumped at the first opportunity to leave before resolving her feelings about her boss.

Every party to an employment decision is obligated to discern the issues of purpose. Purpose raises the questions of competency and compatibility. Failing to ask these questions raises the possibility of termination of employment and termination of relationships.

EXPRESSED VALUE

The interview is the first opportunity the employer has to demonstrate the practice of expressed value. John could have conveyed to Carol his high value for her by conducting a thorough search. The fact that she was the only person interviewed for the position should have raised the red flag that John was engaged in a flippant process.

How would it feel to know you were chosen for a position because of your place in line? Timing is important, but timing has nothing to do with your unique abilities and passions. Investing the time to ensure the right person is fitted and selected for the position is an expression that the person possesses unique abilities. Affirming a person's uniqueness is an expression of value.

John missed an opportunity to express value to his current staff. A well-planned, deliberate search for the most competent and compatible person sends a message to the troops that the boss cares about them. He makes an effort to associate people who will take their place and compliment the team because he highly values the current staff.

Carol could have expressed value to John by raising the question of how her ability fit with the requirements of the job. Such a discussion would have implied Carol's interest in being the right fit to help John move in the direction of his purpose. Helping others understand and follow their purpose is an expression of value.

SERVICE

Focusing on the needs of others is the prerequisite for service. Unfortunately, many people lose the service perspective when it is needed the most. Carol needed John to serve her during the employment decision process. John could have asked, "If I were Carol, what would I want to know, see, and experience in order to make an informed and objective judgment about this company?" Had he asked that question in preparation for Carol's interview, John might have offered her the company personnel manual and scheduled several employees to give Carol a tour, allowing Carol the opportunity to ask them questions. If he had approached the interview with a service mind-set, he certainly would have determined the detailed requirements of the position and offered Carol a written job description. Had he focused on Carol's needs, he would have researched the opportunity and known the shipping costs made the idea barely attractive. Had he looked beyond the obvious, he would have canceled the interview, knowing the opportunity was not worth risking his or Carol's future.

John is not the only culprit in this employment mess. Carol missed the opportunity to serve John. What if Carol had asked questions like: "What could I do to enhance the value of this company? What do you (John) consider to be incredible sales results?" Had Carol asked herself and John those questions, she might have forced him to focus on the detail of the position and led him to see the obstacles before she accepted the position. John was in need of that kind of service.

COMMUNICATION

Poor communication is found at the root of most employment disasters. John and Carol's is a case of virtually no communication. John waxed on and on about his company and the opportunity before them. Carol just sat there and heard only what she wanted to hear.

John spoke almost 80 percent of their time together during the interview. The ultimate result of John and Carol's employment decision might have proven more positive had Carol spoken 80 percent of the time and John 20 percent of the time. John likes to hear himself talk. Solomon warned against such arrogance, "A fool finds no pleasure in understanding but delights in airing his own opinions" (Prov. 18:2). John should have listened to Carol.

John and Carol left the interview with differing expectations. John was impressed that Carol had achieved so much in her computer sales position and felt there was no reason she could not have the same experience with his firm. John was also impressed by Carol's eagerness, but once again John's reaction was off base. Had John probed just a little deeper, he might have concluded Carol's eagerness was the result of her desire to leave her current position more than her desire to work for John. But John wagged his tongue, never giving Carol an opportunity to ask him questions.

Carol left the meeting thinking all the research pointed to a viable business opportunity. She could have asked to read the analysis of the facts. Asking John for that study in an interview situation would have been a gutsy move, but it is exactly these gutsy questions that excite the kind of manager Carol likes. If she had asked the question, she would have learned the study did not exist; and armed with that knowledge, Carol may have made a different decision.

PROMISE KEEPING

Either you keep your promises or you do not. John did not keep his promises to Carol. John implied he had researched the business, and he promised regular performance evaluations. These promises, along with her situation at the computer firm, induced Carol to take the job. We know he broke his promise about the research, and now we learn he broke his promise about regular performance evaluations. In the short period of time Carol worked for John, he never constructively evaluated her performance. John was quick to let Carol know he was not pleased with her performance, but a meeting to discuss her approach to the business and suggest different ways she might approach the business never happened.

INTEGRITY

People of character run a different race. The only standard we measure ourselves against is our purpose and our practice. In the lonely solitude preceding the decision to fire an employee or an employer, we must ask the hard questions to make sure we have followed our purpose and desired practice. If we can truly say we have lived out our purpose and desired practice, then we can approach the firing with confidence, knowing we have given the person an advantage to make or exceed his or her goals and we are making a decision that is in the other person's best interest.

John did not stop to think through Carol's situation. He acted out of his emotion instead of acting out of his will. He decided Carol needed to go, and he harshly delivered the news a few minutes later. John would have been wise if he had asked himself the following questions:

- Did I provide Carol all the necessary training and resources?
- Did I clearly define her role and my expectations for her performance?
- Is Carol a good fit for another job in my company?
- Am I committed to Carol?
- What is best for Carol?

These questions are not a test that can be totaled and an objective decision reached about employment status. The questions provide a framework to ensure you are prudently, objectively approaching a difficult employment decision, a decision to fire an employee or employer. These questions help bring perspective to what could be an emotionally charged decision. These questions are intended to help you maintain your integrity to your purpose and desired practice.

HIRING AND FIRING AND THE CHARACTER EQUATION

1. When a friend calls for advice with an employment decision, how will you answer the question, What should I do?
2. How can you express value to others through the employment process?
3. List questions you might ask when making an employment decision.

TWENTY

The Power of Zero

I wandered through life for a number of years doing "just enough to get by." I was part of the unfulfilled 80 percent. So many other people were wandering the same road it seemed like the right place to be, but the still small voice of my soul cried out for change. Early one morning I peered into the mirror. I was eye to eye with myself as I pondered this thought, *You have worked hard to achieve certain goals, and you are succeeding. Your life is probably about 50 percent lived. What of lasting significance do you have to show for it?*

I was running in the middle of the pack of the masses, and all I could see around me were other runners. I could see how the others were running their races. I could compare my distance, speed, and stamina; but those comparisons were not fulfilling. I knew there was more to life than the aimless race I was running, but I did not know where a more fulfilling, significant race might be run or how to get there.

That very powerful day at my mortgage company office revealed the hopelessness of running a race based on self-gratification and self-indulgence. I saw myself in many of the people I encountered that day, forcing me to acknowledge the futility of continuing my current practice of life. I saw the personal devastation such a race had caused in so many lives, and I knew this race would consume me too.

That important day at the mortgage company revealed the link between purpose and practice. I knew about purpose in life. I have sensed a purpose for many years (since the day I believed in God), but I failed to establish the link between my purpose and my practice. My actions spoke loudly saying, "There is no connection between my purpose and my practice of life." I discovered I was unfulfilled because I was not practicing my purpose.

The character equation was conceived that day. I wrote my discovery in the form of an equation so I would remember it: Character = Purpose x Practice. For the first time in years I was hopeful of finally enjoying fulfillment, stability, and meaning. The ten practices were distilled from centuries-old wisdom (Scripture) and added to bring a practical picture of how to live out the purpose. The equation kept me focused on the right race, but I sensed the equation was not yet complete.

A NEW STANDARD

I worked on the development of a program for leaders of business, government, and organizations with Jim Standard, an Atlanta businessman.[1] We met on a Wednesday in early June and agreed to get together again the next Monday. As I was packing my car for the three-hour drive home, Jim lingered with me longer than usual. It was as if he wanted to tell me something but did not know what to say. He stalled my departure several times saying, "Oh, one more thing."

Two days later, Friday morning, a friend called with an untimely message, "Jim Standard died this morning." I believe Jim's still small voice had whispered to him that his days were numbered. I believe he sensed a finality to our meeting, and so he lingered a moment or two longer. I am glad he did.

Moses teaches us a great lesson for life. He wrote, "Teach us to number our days aright, that we may gain a heart of wisdom" (Ps. 90:12). Moses looked back over his incredible life and reduced all his experience and knowledge into this simple verse which challenges us to practice life "aright" every day.

We practice life simply by living. Every day our practice is defined by our choices, decisions, and attitudes. We control our practice, and we have the choice to practice life "aright" every day, and we have the choice simply to wander along unanchored, without direction every day. Life is lived one day at a time, and Moses reminds us to make each day count.

The daily practice of life is different from practicing life "aright" every day. Practicing life "aright" each day suggests a specific pattern of living based on unchanging principles. Practicing life "aright" each day implies the principled life is headed for a specific destination, a reward for a life well lived. Practicing life "aright" each day accomplishes a purpose.

Moses linked the daily practice of life "aright" and purpose in life, writing, "May the favor of the Lord our God rest upon us; establish the work of our hands for us—yes, establish the work of our hands" (Ps. 90:17). Combining these two powerful, practical, and purposeful verses, we learn that practicing life "aright" every day leads us to establish the "work of our hands." Practice your purpose every day, and at the end of your life you will have accomplished your purpose. Common sense, yes. But is this the common practice of your life?

Jim Standard, Moses, and others helped me understand that the missing variable of the character equation is time. I ran the wrong race for so long because I said, "Well, I have plenty of time to connect all the dots. For now I will continue life as I know it." I remained unfulfilled. I needed a catalyst to shock me into action. Jim Standard, Moses, and others were my catalysts.

As a reminder of the importance of time in the context of the character equation, I turn to Psalm 90 every year on my birthday. On that page of my Bible, you will find a series of numbers. Each year I calculate the number of days between my current age and 70 years. (Seventy years is mentioned in Psalm 90, and my dad died at age 70.) Next I multiply 365 days per year times the number of years to age 70. Take a 40-year-old person and subtract the age from 70. You have 30 years X 365 which equals 10,950 days. That means I have 10,950 days to practice a purposeful life, but that sounds like a long time to me. I worry that I could fall back to my old habit of saying I will get around to practicing a purposeful life "someday." So I recalculate the number of days between my current age and the age my grandfathers died. Both of my grandfathers died in their mid-forties. So 45 minus 40 equals 5 x 365 equals 1,825. Wow! That is not very many days to enjoy the fulfillment of a purposefully practiced life, but I still worry about my tendency to fall back into that "someday" mode. So I remember Jim Standard. I was with Jim one day, and less than 48 hours later without warning he was gone. I was reminded, as I have been reminded over and over, that all we really have is today. This insight helped me complete the character equation.

CHARACTER = (PURPOSE X PRACTICE)^0

The character equation is completed by raising the entire equation to the power of zero. What is the answer whenever an equation is raised to the power of zero? The answer is always one! Raising the equation to the power of zero brings time and perspective into the equation. Now raised to the power of zero, the character equation provides a sense of urgency because we only have one day, one purpose, and often one opportunity.

ONE DAY

Friday morning did not dawn for Jim Standard. Jim was not here to see our plans implemented. The only thing that mattered to Jim on his last day was who he loved, who loved him, and if he had practiced a purposeful life.

Tuesday, March 21, 1989, at 2 P.M. my father ended his earthbound journey. Gathered around his hospital bed at that moment, we recalled the many ways Dad practiced his purpose every day. We knew his cancer-ridden body could not hold off the certain outcome of the disease. We thought we were prepared for his death, but the day he died we were in shock.

Even though we knew Dad's death was near, we were reminded that knowledge without experience is limited understanding. Only when we experience the horror of losing a best friend and father can we truly understand the depth of that loss. The same is true with purpose. Only when we practice our purpose every day do we truly understand its depth and meaning.

The only day we are certain of is today. If tomorrow did not dawn for you, would your life have been purposeful?

ONE PURPOSE

In the movie *City Slickers,* Curly asks, "What is the meaning of life? Then he holds up one finger and says, "One thing." Mitch asks, "What is it?" and Curly says, "You have to find that out for yourself."

Like Curly, I am not going to tell you what your purpose is in life. You will have to find that out for yourself, using the helps provided in this book. I will, however, give you hope. You do have a purpose, a glorious purpose. Choosing to practice a life inconsistent with your purpose is to choose to miss the fulfillment, stability, and meaning your soul desires.

ONE OPPORTUNITY

Each Christmas we string little white lights around and around and around our tree. Anticipating a beautifully lit tree, we plug in the cord and one light on one string has burned out. The lights down line from the burned out bulb cannot do their job. They are zapped of the power necessary to bring them life. People are like that, too. We are like lights on a Christmas tree string. When one of us burns out and when we miss the opportunity to practice our purpose in the life of another, we impact the whole string. People miss the power of encouragement that comes from a person practicing a purposeful life.

We are like links in a chain and dominoes in a line and legs of a stool and lights of a tree. When we fail to practice a purposeful life every day, the chain gets a little weaker. When we wander without purpose, we are subject to the often harsh winds of life; and like a domino standing on its end, we are easily toppled. Our fall affects the entire line. When our feet are not squarely planted in our purpose, we wobble, and this affects the other legs of the stool.

We have but one day to practice our one purpose and often only one opportunity to value, encourage, and learn from others. One opportunity to demonstrate a balanced life, hold others accountable, and be of service to those in need. We may have only one opportunity to communicate with someone, to be a promise keeper and wise steward. We may have but one opportunity to maintain our integrity.

My most treasured Olympic memory occurred in the 1992 summer games. Derrick Redmond of Great Britain was one of the competitors in the four-hundred-meter race. This race is a tough event because you sprint the entire race. Derrick fell as he rounded a curve. His hamstring pulled, and in intense pain, Derrick hobbled to his feet and started limping to the finish line. One official tried to stop him, but Derrick pushed him off. Suddenly a spectator jumped from the stands and onto the track and placed his arm around Derrick. It took the pair five minutes, but they finished the race! The world watched as these men crossed the finish line. The media engulfed them, asking the spectator why he did it. The man replied, "I am Derrick's dad. We started this race together, and we are going to finish this race together."

We are running this race of life together. People all around you are limping along, hobbled by the pain life can bring. Practice your purpose and pick them up. Coworkers are on the brink of unemployment, and they need your help to find stability. Practice your purpose. Family members are wondering what and who are really important to you. Practice your purpose. We have one day to practice our one purpose, taking advantage of often one opportunity.

TODAY IS THE DAY

The time to begin practicing your purpose is now, today. Here are three ways to get started:

1. Understand your purpose. Spend time considering your purpose. The early chapters of this book are designed to lead you through the process. Begin writing your purpose statement. It will take time and energy to capture your purpose in a single statement, but the rewards are eternal.
2. Establish and practice measurable actions. I am certain coworkers, family members, and friends have come to mind as you have read this book. Maybe there is a measurable action you can take in their lives

to practice your purpose. Perhaps this action involves expressed value or learning or any of the ten practices. Whatever the actions, write them down and create a checklist as accountability to begin practicing your purpose. Establish the process of identifying and recording measurable actions as your ongoing pattern of practicing a purposeful life.

3. Burn the ships. The explorer Cortés sailed from Cuba in search of new lands in 1519. Cortés and his men were looking for new life—a better life. He landed in Mexico and met resistance. Life was hard, and some of his men wanted to sail back to Cuba and their life of safety and comfort. But Cortés had a different idea. He told his men to burn the ships because they were not going back.[2]

Cortés freed his men to practice their purpose by removing the temptation to abandon their purpose. He knew his men could not truly live until they had confronted the reality that they might die. The ships represented a safe escape, and as long as it existed his men could not fight with passion and intensity.

It has been said that "we are not ready to live until we are ready to die." We cannot enjoy the fulfillment, stability, and meaning a life of character offers until we are willing to die to our own desires. What obstacles exist that hinder your purposeful practice? Perhaps you too must burn some ships.

Character is much more than the total qualities of a person's life. Character is the strength to practice a purposeful life every day! Such a life will not force itself on you, but this life of fulfillment, stability, and meaning desires to be the choice of all people. Living a life of character is your decision. It is said that Alexander was Great because "he acted without delay." Will you?

Endnotes

CHAPTER 1

1. Marjorie Kelly, "Was 1996 the Year without Employees?" *Business Ethics,* March/April 1997, 5.
2. Henry David Thoreau, "Economy," *Walden.*
3. *Business Ethics,* March/April 1997, 16.

CHAPTER 3

1. Dietrich Bonhoeffer, *The Cost of Discipleship* (New York: Simon & Schuster, 1959), 15.
2. "Millard Fuller," Habitat for Humanity Website.

CHAPTER 4

1. Gary Smalley and John Trent, *The Two Sides of Love* (Colorado Springs: Focus on the Family, 1990), 7.
2. "Officers Give Off Time to Peer with Sick Child," Gannett News Service.
3. William J. Bennett, *The Book of Virtues* (New York: Simon & Schuster, 1993), 269.

CHAPTER 5

1. Daniel J. Conti and Wayne N. Burton, "The Economic Impact of Depression in the Workplace," *Journal of Medicine,* 36 (1994), 983.
2. Hal Lancaster, "Managing Your Career," *The Wall Street Journal,* 26 August 1997, B1.
3. For information about FCCI, contact The WorkLife Company at 800-383-2653.

CHAPTER 6

1. Marjorie Kelly, "Was 1996 the Year without Employees?" *Business Ethics,* March/April 1997, 5.
2. Robert McMath, *What Were They Thinking?* (New York: Random House, 1998), 32.
3. Kenneth Labich, "Why Companies Fail," *Fortune,* 14 November 1994, 58.
4. R. H. Al-Mabuk and R. D. Enright, "Forgiveness Education with Parentally Love-deprived Late Adolescents," *Journal of Moral Education,* 24:4 (1995), 427–44.
5. Trudy Tynan, "Judge Orders Man to Wear Patriots Cap as Penance," *The Montgomery Advertiser,* 20 April 1995, 6A.

CHAPTER 7

1. Stephanie Armour, "Blame It on Downsizing, E-mail, Laptops and Dual-career Families," *USA Today*, 13 March 1998, 1B.
2. Ibid.
3. Ramona Richards, "Held Hostage by the American Dream," *HomeLife*, April 1998, 21.
4. Ibid.
5. "Americans Fatter Than Ever, Study Says," *The Montgomery Advertiser*, 26 November 1996, 2A.
6. 1993 Promise Keepers Conference, Boulder, Colorado.

CHAPTER 8

1. "Declining Values: Myth or Reality?" *The Numbers News*, December 1995, 5.
2. Mary Glynn Peeples, *All We Like Sheep* (Birmingham, Ala.: The Sheep Shoppe, 1987), 51–52.
3. "Problem Pupils Excel with Expectations," *Montgomery Advertiser*, 4 July 1996, 6A.

CHAPTER 9

1. Bill Evans, "Notes & Deeds," *Perspectives*, November 1991, 11.

CHAPTER 10

1. Tammy Joyner, "Working Things Out," *The Atlanta Constitution*, 28 October 1996, 1E.
2. Everett R. Robinson, *Why Aren't You More Like Me?* (Suma, Wash.: CR Press, 1997), 196–97.
3. Gary Smalley and John Trent, *The Two Sides of Love* (Colorado Springs: Focus on the Family, 1990), 35.
4. For more information on these profiling systems contact The WorkLife Company at 800-383-2653 or write at P.O. Box 11328, Montgomery, AL 36111.
5. Cynthia Ulrich Tobias, *The Way We Work* (Colorado Springs: Focus on the Family, 1995), 12.

CHAPTER 11

1. For more information about the WorldCulture Profile, contact The WorkLife Company at 800-383-2653.
2. Shari Caudron, "Blowing the Whistle—Alternative Dispute Resolution," *WorkForce*, May 1997, 52.
3. Oswald Chambers, *My Utmost for His Highest*, Oswald Chambers Publications Association, Ltd., 9 December 1995.

CHAPTER 12

1. "Firms Take New Look at Sick Days," *USA Today*, 8 October 1996, 8B.
2. Leslie Alderman, "What You Need to Do to Get More Money from Your Boss," *Money*, January 1995, 34.
3. "Good Works, Good Business," *USA Today*, 25 April 1997, 1B.
4. Ibid.

5. Ibid.

6. "Companies Put Time, Not Money, into Problems," *Montgomery Advertiser*, 22 April 1997, 5E.

7. "Good Works, Good Business," *USA Today,* 25 April 1997, 1B.

CHAPTER 13

1. Lucette Lagnado, "Hospitals Profit by 'Upcoding' Illness," *Wall Street Journal*, 17 April 1997, B1.

2. Amy Kuebelbeck, "Tobacco Firm Memo: 'Bury' Unfavorable Research," *The Atlanta Constitution*, 18 September 1996, A6.

3. "Balancing Ethics and Technology," *USA Today*, 27 April 1998, 1A.

4. Del Jones, "Doing the Wrong Thing," *USA Today*, 4–6 April 1997, 1A.

5. James Patterson and Peter Kim, *The Day America Told the Truth* (New York: Plume Publishing, 1992), 65.

6. Michael Ryan, "They Call Their Boss a Hero," *Parade Magazine*, 4 September 1996, 4.

CHAPTER 14

1. "Warning Signs," *Business Ethics*, November/December 1996, 8.

CHAPTER 15

1. Gillian Flynn, "Why Employees Are So Angry?" *WorkForce*, September 1998, 27.

2. Ibid.

CHAPTER 17

1. Harriet Rubin, "Success and Excess," *Fast Company*, October 1998, 110.

2. Ibid., 112.

3. Harriet Rubin, "Art of Darkness," *Fast Company*, October 1998, 132.

4. *Mickey Mantle: His Final Inning*, American Tract Society, 1995.

5. Gerry Spence, "Gerry Spence's Liberty!" interview with Greta Van Susteran and Roger Cossack, *Burden of Proof*, 25 December 1998.

CHAPTER 18

1. Michael Josephson, "Making Ethics Part of Our Business," *Mortgage Originator*, December 1994, 9.

2. "Would You Lie to Save Your Company?" *Inc.*, October 1998, 136.

3. George Anthan, "Former ADM Executives Found Guilty in Lysine Price-fixing," *Des Moines Register*, 27 September 1998, 1.

4. Dale Kurschner, "5 Ways Ethical Business Creates Fatter Profits," *Business Ethics*, March/April 1996, 21.

5. For more information, contact The WorkLife Company at 800-383-2653.

CHAPTER 20

1. For more information on this program, call WorkLife at 800-383-2653.

2. Beatrice Berler, *The Conquest of Mexico* (San Antonio: Corona Publishing Company, 1988), 28.

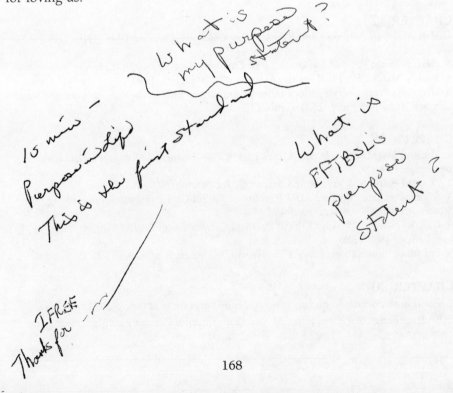

Acknowledgments

This book is the product of years of working with thousands of men and women in corporate settings who desire not merely to make a living but to make a life. Thank you for your honesty, energy, and passion.

Ken Stephens, Bucky Rosenbaum, Leonard Goss, John Landers, and Sandy Bryer at Broadman & Holman captured the vision for this book and worked tirelessly to help pull it together. It is a privilege to be on your team, and I am thankful you are on mine.

Mark and Chris Anderson, Steve and Elizabeth Barrington, Jim Ellick, Minnie Lamberth, Steve and Connie Tucker, Bob and Eileen Raun, and Danny and Gwen Mairs provided unconditional friendship and insight. Thanks.

And to Jerry and Becky Washington, my incredible in-laws. Thank you for loving us.